Living in the
ELEVENTH
HOUR

Living in the ELEVENTH HOUR

Preparing for the
Glorious Return of the Savior

ROBERT L. MILLET

DESERET
BOOK

Salt Lake City, Utah

Library of Congress Cataloging-in-Publication Data

CIP data on file
ISBN 978-1-60907-409-8

Printed in the United States of America
Edwards Brothers Malloy, Ann Arbor, MI

10   9   8   7   6   5   4   3   2   1

Wherefore the voice of the Lord is unto the ends of the earth, that all that will hear may hear: Prepare ye, prepare ye for that which is to come, for the Lord is nigh.

Doctrine & Covenants 1:11–12

CONTENTS

PREFACE

Some of the earliest memories of my childhood are of long gospel conversations between my father and my uncle Joseph. Dad had a near obsession with the postmortal spirit world, and Uncle Joseph loved to read and talk about the signs of the times, those prophetic warnings and signals of the Savior's second coming. My cousin Linda and I sat for scores of hours through the years, drinking in all that our two gospel heroes discussed. We heard of wars and thunder and lightning and false prophets and the moon turning to blood and the stars falling from heaven. We sat in awe and wonder as we heard of the cleansing of the earth by fire, the destruction of the wicked, the Lord and his faithful Saints descending to earth, and on and on. On the one hand, these ideas thrilled us; on the other hand, to be honest, there were times when we walked away from the conversations some- what frightened.

For some reason, as a young boy I thought a great deal about the Second Coming, wondering when it would be, puzzling over who of those I knew would be spared and who would die. And I worried over what camp I would fit into—the redeemed or the destroyed. I can still remember thinking about these things quite frequently on Sunday evenings as our family drove home from church, a distance of some thirty or forty miles. I also remember having more than one nightmare about the Second Coming, about the terror in the eyes of those who were unprepared, about people coming up out of their graves. As a kid I was fixated on science fiction and horror movies, so you can appreciate just how ghoulish and graphic those dreams were!

By the time I was a young teenager, the Lord's coming in glory was something that horrified me, something I wanted to avoid entirely, if at all possible. In other words, fear and serious apprehension characterized my views of the Master's second advent. I wasn't ready for that *terrible* day—I hadn't had a chance to live my life yet, and even what little bit I had been able to live was anything but perfect.

As the years have passed, as I have had occasion to read and study and ponder on the revelations of the Restoration and as I have been buffeted by the stresses and disappointments, the traumas and tragedies, of this telestial world, the Second Coming has become more and more attractive. I have found myself looking forward to that day when evil men and seducers will no longer be able to confuse and distract the unwary; when honesty and decency will be the norm in society; when mischief and deceit will be entirely done away; when disease and pain and death and family distress will have become a distant memory; when our missionaries will be permitted to teach the principles of the restored gospel far and wide; when the Lord Jesus Christ will reign and preach and dwell among his people on earth; and, in the words of the ancient prophets, when the knowledge of God will cover the earth as the waters cover the sea (Habakkuk 2:14; Isaiah 11:9). In short, I long now for that *great* day.

We live in what some have called the eleventh hour of time,

the last days, the final period of preparation before the "Master of ocean and earth and skies" returns to once again subdue the raging tempest.[1] We of the eleventh hour live in a unique time: We can read the scriptures and realize that much of what was prophesied to take place before our Lord's return in glory *has in fact already taken place*. But we also are aware of many significant events that are yet to be acted out on earth's stage, many great and many terrible things. And so with prophecy that is now history right before our eyes, as it were, we have certain assurance that what Jesus Christ and his anointed servants have spoken relative to the Second Coming is indeed true: It has already come to pass! We have every reason therefore to have perfect confidence in holy writ, every reason to trust that what has not yet occurred will in fact come to pass. We are called upon, therefore, to live our lives in readiness, to be vigilant, ever anticipating the ushering in of the millennial day.

This work has been written with those events in mind. My intention is not to frighten but to fortify; not to startle but to solidify; not to be sensational but to be sound. My hope is to remind us of prophetic principles we need to *know*, the deeds of discipleship we need to *do*, and, perhaps most important, the kind of person we need to *become* in order to feel peaceful and prepared when the Savior returns in glory.

ACKNOWLEDGMENTS

No work of this kind comes to fruition without the assistance of many persons. Students and faculty colleagues through the years have challenged me in my thinking and teaching and motivated me to search the revelations and the prophets more thoroughly to obtain a clearer picture of the way things are and the way they will be.

In the preparation of the manuscript, I am especially appreciative of the encouragement and aid offered by Lisa Roper, Chris Schoebinger, and Heidi Taylor of Deseret Book Company, who have shepherded this project along. And as always, I thank my editor and friend Suzanne Brady, whose suggestions and recommendations, as well as her sharp and discerning editorial eye, have simply made this book better than it would otherwise have been.

Finally, I express my deep love and appreciation for Shauna, my beloved wife, companion, and best friend, whose goodness and compassion have inspired me for almost half a century. She has been the quiet but compelling influence behind all that I have accomplished in this life that is of any lasting value.

Chapter 1

WHILE IT IS CALLED TODAY

*W*e sing in our sacrament services a beloved hymn that begins with these lines:

> *Jesus, once of humble birth,*
> *Now in glory comes to earth.*
> *Once he suffered grief and pain;*
> *Now he comes on earth to reign.*[1]

Jesus Christ is coming to earth, this time not as the lowly Nazarene but as the returning King of Israel (John 1:49), the King of Zion (Moses 7:53), the Lord of Sabaoth (Lord of Hosts, Lord of Armies). He will come with his angels, his destroying angels: "For behold, the day cometh that shall burn as an oven, and all the proud, yea, and all that do wickedly shall burn as stubble; for *they that come shall burn them*, saith the Lord of Hosts, that it shall leave them neither root nor branch" (Joseph Smith–History 1:37; emphasis added). This scene will be what the scriptures call the "end of the world," meaning the end of the worldly or the destruction of the wicked (Joseph Smith–Matthew 1:4). It has been described as a day that is both great and dreadful: great for those who are prepared to receive him, and dreadful for those who would prefer that the Master postpone his coming indefinitely.

The Second Coming is not something we need fear or be unduly alarmed about. It can and should be a glorious and long-awaited day for men and women who have grown weary of waywardness, who have had their patience stretched by the allurements and tauntings of a world engulfed in wickedness. It will be a time of deliverance and salvation, a day of joy and sweet satisfaction, particularly for those who have watched for his coming and sought to stand in holy places.

Yes, the Lord is coming. And when is he coming? President Joseph Fielding Smith explained: "I was asked, not long ago, if I could tell when the Lord would come. I answered, Yes; and I answer, Yes, now. I know when he will come. He will come *tomorrow*. We have his word for it. Let me read it:

"'Behold, *now it is called today until the coming of the Son of Man,* and verily it is a day of sacrifice, and a day for the tithing of my people; for he that is tithed shall not be burned at his coming.' (Now there is a discourse sufficient on tithing.) 'For *after today cometh the burning*—this is speaking after the manner of the Lord—for verily I say, *tomorrow all the proud and they that do wickedly shall be as stubble;* and I will burn them up, for I am the Lord of Hosts; and I will not spare any that remain in Babylon' [D&C 64:23–24; see also 45:61; Malachi 3:2; 4:1].

"So the Lord is coming, I say, *tomorrow.* Then let us be prepared. Elder Orson F. Whitney used to write about the *Saturday Evening of Time.* . . . This is the 6th day now drawing to its close. When the Lord says it is today until his coming, that, I think, is what he has in mind, for *he shall come in the morning of the Sabbath, or seventh day* of the earth's temporal existence, to inaugurate the millennial reign and to take his rightful place as King of kings and Lord of lords, to rule and reign upon the earth, as it is his right [see D&C 77:12]."[2]

The greatest preparation we can make today as we anticipate tomorrow is to attend to the small and simple things that come before us each minute and hour of every day. Abraham was able to surrender his own will to Jehovah and to do the unthinkable—offer his son Isaac in sacrifice—because of the hundreds of private battles of the soul he had waged and won. In our own lives there are moments that matter, significant times in which choices are made between self-denial and self-absorption, struggles of the soul that call for mere meekness rather than railing accusation, conflagrations that require schooling the feelings rather than exploding in anger and resentment. Public success is always preceded by private victories won within individual human hearts.

The extent to which I am prepared to meet the Lord Jesus when he comes again might very well be reflected, for example, in the extent to which I am learning each day to tame the tongue; to channel my thoughts in righteous paths; to choose not to be offended but rather to assume the best; to ask myself consistently what I can do to serve and lighten the burdens of others; to put on hold my immediate gratification in order to achieve a higher aim than satisfied selfhood; to be willing to be inconvenienced; and to be found at my duty station at all times.

The prophet-writer Mormon spoke to his beloved son Moroni near the time of the destruction of the Nephite nation (in the fifth century after the coming of Christ) of those about him who "have lost their love, one towards another; and they thirst after blood and revenge continually." Mormon then delivered this noble charge: "And now, my beloved son, notwithstanding their hardness, *let us labor diligently*; for if we should cease to labor, we should be brought under condemnation; *for we have a labor to perform whilst in this tabernacle of clay, that we may conquer the enemy of all righteousness, and rest our souls in the kingdom of God"* (Moroni 9:5–6; emphasis added).

And so it is with us in the twenty-first century. We too have a labor to perform. We too must conquer Satan, the enemy of all righteousness, so that we too may rest our souls in the kingdom of God and enjoy life on a celestialized earth with God and Christ and our families forevermore.

Chapter 2

"UPON MY HOUSE SHALL IT BEGIN"

In writing to the early Christians scattered throughout the Roman Empire, the apostle Peter spoke more than once of the challenges that lay ahead, the persecution they would face, the corruption within the Church that would continue to grow: "Beloved, think it not strange concerning the fiery trial which is to try you, as though some strange thing happened unto you: but rejoice, inasmuch as ye are partakers of Christ's sufferings; that, when his glory shall be revealed, ye may be glad also with exceeding joy" (1 Peter 4:12–13).

In other words, it should have been no surprise to the disciples of the Master that trials and traumas were to be a part of their future, that if one coveted the glory and blessings hereafter, one must be willing to be a partaker of the fellowship of Christ's sufferings here (compare Romans 8:11; 2 Corinthians 1:7). Peter's counsel continued: "Yet if any man suffer as a Christian, let him not be ashamed; but let him glorify God on this behalf." Then came what must have been a rather chilling warning, one that no doubt sobered the Saints: "For the time is come that *judgment must begin at the house of God:* and if it first begin at us, what shall the end be of them that obey not the gospel of God? And if

5

the righteous scarcely be saved, where shall the ungodly and the sinner appear?" (1 Peter 4:16–18; emphasis added).

"Judgment must begin at the house of God." This is a stunning statement, one that reminds me of what Jesus said in his denunciation of the hypocrisy and self-righteousness of the Pharisees and scribes: "Ye blind guides, who strain at a gnat, and swallow a camel; who make yourselves appear unto men that ye would not commit the least sin, and yet ye yourselves, transgress the whole law. Woe unto you, scribes and Pharisees, hypocrites! For ye make clean the outside of the cup, and of the platter; but *within they are full of extortion and excess*. Ye blind Pharisees! *Cleanse first the cup and platter within*, that the outside of them may be clean also" (JST, Matthew 23:21–23; emphasis added).

I remember very well when I was first called to serve as a bishop. The call was not a total surprise, since I had awakened a few months earlier in the middle of the night with a sense that such an assignment was on the way. Even so, I began to feel the weight of the task once the stake president invited me into his office and extended the call.

After the sacrament meeting in which I was sustained and after shaking hands with many of the ward members (this was before the consolidated meeting schedule had been introduced to the Church), we made our way into the high council room for the ordination and setting apart. I recall what a sweet occasion it was, since my parents were visiting us and Dad was invited to stand in the circle. The stake president first ordained me to the office of bishop, then set me apart as the bishop of that particular ward, and began to pronounce a blessing. There were many things spoken concerning unusual opportunities the Lord would provide for me that, as I thought about them, reached well beyond my years of service as bishop. I sensed the power of the priesthood of these noble men as their hands rested upon my head, sensed that the Lord approved of what was being done, and felt an appreciable amount of anxiety dissipate as the blessing proceeded.

All was peaceful and positive and edifying until the stake president, one of the most Christlike men I have ever known, said in essence, "Now, Bishop Millet, you are called to preside over a ward of very good people, men and women who love the Lord and are earnestly striving to keep his commandments. But there is a great deal of sin among some of your flock, serious sin that can only be dealt with through Church discipline. Search it out, deal with it, and lives will be enriched—the spirituality of your ward will increase dramatically."

That hard counsel was both true and prophetic: I spent several weeks, with my counselors, getting to know the ward members better, including inviting many of those who were either less active or disgruntled into my office so that I could take the spiritual temperature of the congregation. In the process and in confidential settings, many men and women who had carried the heavy burden of sin, some for decades, confessed their misdeeds, were placed on the path of faith and repentance, and in some cases submitted themselves to Church discipline. And, as the stake president had predicted, the love of God and the peace that flows from reconciliation and forgiveness were forthcoming in a manner that greater light and more peaceful countenances were apparent.

I have, since that time, marveled at how applicable a passage in the Book of Mormon was to our particular situation. You will recall in the Nephite narrative that Captain Moroni, frustrated because his requests for provisions and additional soldiers seemed to be ignored and recognizing that no doubt there was corruption within the government, wrote a stinging letter of rebuke to the chief judge, Pahoran. "Do ye suppose that God will look upon you as guiltless while ye sit still and behold these things?" Moroni asked. "Behold I say unto you, Nay. Now I would that ye should remember that *God has said that the inward vessel shall be cleansed first,* and then shall the outer vessel be cleansed also" (Alma 60:23; emphasis added).

These sentiments are not unrelated to Jesus' parable of the wheat and the tares (Matthew 13:24–30, 36–43). A field of wheat was planted. During the night an enemy quietly invaded the field and sowed tares—darnel grass, noxious weeds—among the wheat. As the plants began to grow, they all looked much the same. But as time passed, it became apparent that something was wrong, that mischief was afoot, and that the field no longer consisted solely of wheat plants. Should those who tend the field root up the tares so that the wheat might grow unhampered? Probably not, since such an effort might well result in wheat being uprooted as well, because the plants were still to some extent indistinguishable. The decision: Wait until the harvest, and then the wheat would be gathered out and stored in the garners, whereas the tares would be bound in bundles and burned.

This is, of course, our situation in the Church today. There are tares among the wheat, men and women who are steeped in sin, while others are bent on embarrassing or even destroying the restored Church. The scriptural counsel in modern revelation is clear: "Pluck not up the tares while the blade is yet tender (for verily your faith is weak), lest you destroy the wheat also. Therefore, let the wheat and the tares grow together until the harvest is fully ripe"—which is the second coming of the Savior, what the scriptures call the "end of the world, or the destruction of the wicked" (Joseph Smith–Matthew 1:4)—"then ye shall first gather out the wheat from among the tares, and after the gathering of the wheat, behold and lo, the tares are bound in bundles, and the field remaineth to be burned" (D&C 86:7).

We do not excommunicate every person in the Church who is engulfed in sin, nor do we always cut off those who revel in dissent, who feel some sense of divine call to steady the ark and put the Church back on course, who deny the truth and defy the counsel of its leaders. In speaking to Church educators, President Boyd K. Packer recalled a conversation with President Henry D. Moyle: "We were driving back from Arizona and were talking about a man who destroyed the faith of young people from the vantage point of a teaching position. Someone asked President Moyle why this man was still a member of the Church when he did things like that. 'He is not a member of the Church,' President Moyle answered firmly. Another replied that he had not heard of his excommunication. 'He has excommunicated himself,' President Moyle responded. 'He has cut himself off from the Spirit of God. Whether or not we get around to holding a [council] doesn't matter that much; he has cut himself off from the Spirit of the Lord.'"[1]

One day Christ the King will come again, this time in glory and might and majesty. He will "gather together my people, according to the parable of the wheat and the tares, that the wheat may be secured in the garners to possess eternal life, and be crowned with celestial glory, when I shall come in the kingdom of my Father to reward every man according as his work shall be; while the tares shall be bound in bundles, and their bands made strong, that they may be burned with unquenchable fire" (D&C 101:65–66). In that day he will cleanse the inner vessel, will excise from his Church those elements that defile or deter or distract, will separate out those persons whose commitment to the cause of truth has proven to be more pretended than real.

As he declared in our dispensation, "Behold, vengeance cometh speedily upon the inhabitants of the earth, a day of wrath, a day of burning, a day of desolation, of weeping, of mourning, and of lamentation; and as a whirlwind it shall come upon all the face of the earth, saith the Lord. And *upon my house shall it begin, and from my house shall it go forth,* saith the Lord; first among those among you, saith the Lord, who have professed to know my name and have not known me, and have blasphemed against me in the midst of my house" (D&C 112:24–26; emphasis added). For this reason the Lord has commanded: "Sanctify yourselves; gather ye together, O ye people of my church, upon the land of Zion. . . . Go ye out from Babylon. Be ye clean that bear the vessels of the Lord" (D&C 133:4–5).

Paul's counsel to the former-day Saints is timely and timeless: "Finally, brethren, whatsoever things are true, whatsoever things are honest, whatsoever things are just, whatsoever things are pure, whatsoever things are lovely, whatsoever things are of good report; if there be any virtue, and if there be any praise, *think on these things*" (Philippians 4:8; emphasis added). The members of the Church, those who have come out of the world by covenant, must develop a righteous obsession with goodness, must separate themselves from that which defiles, must reject and refuse that which soils the soul, must eschew that which is of the world and thus will be burned by the brightness of the Lord's coming. We must hold tightly and tenaciously to that which will endure everlastingly.

Chapter 3

THE LOVE OF MEN WAXES COLD

I picked up the newspaper some weeks ago and sat down to have breakfast. Between bites of cereal, I noticed a headline about the Federal Communications Commission. It seemed that the FCC had decided that while they want to avoid what they identified as egregious examples of profanity and nudity in television programming, they had tentatively decided to allow more profanity and more female frontal nudity. While I was pleased to learn that 75,000 persons had responded negatively to the announcement, I was disheartened to discover that any sane individual or institution should feel that it's time for America to sink a little lower.

More recently I read on the front page of a newspaper that an abortion doctor had been convicted of murder in the deaths of babies that were delivered alive and then killed at his clinic. He was also found guilty of involuntary manslaughter in the death of a patient. The jury was to decide whether he should receive the death penalty.

In recent years we have heard a great deal about the nation's financial woes, and chief executives, senators and representatives, and economists have had much to say about how to climb out of the economic hole the country has found itself in. In reflecting on how we as a people got where we are now, I have come to believe that our problem is only partially a financial one. Oh, to be sure, we need to make some serious budgetary adjustments in order to recover, but in many ways such efforts are like straightening deck chairs on the Titanic. To use another metaphor, we are, as Thoreau suggested, trimming the leaves of the tree rather than hacking away at the roots. That is, our economic challenges are merely a symptom of far more serious moral problems: gluttony, greed, man's inhumanity to man, and his disregard for his fellows.

It is important to recognize in a new and heartfelt way why the Savior identified the two great commandments as loving God and loving fellow man and that "on these two commandments hang all the law and the prophets" (Matthew 22:35–40). That is to say, everything else is secondary and supplementary. First of all, if we love the Lord our God with all our heart, might, mind, and strength and serve him in the name of Jesus Christ (D&C 59:5), we will in fact be seriously focused on lifting burdens, lightening loads, and offering hope and encouragement to our brothers and sisters about us—all as a part of our Christian covenant responsibility (Mosiah 18:8–10). Why? Simply because, as King Benjamin instructed us, when we are in the service of our fellow beings we are only in the service of our God (Mosiah 2:17). We serve God best when we serve those whom God loves—his children.

So many of earth's problems have arisen because people have chosen either to try to love their fellow mortals without first loving God or to serve humanity when in fact they just can't stand people! The former situation proves deficient at best and perverse at worst: We as fallen creatures simply do not have the strength, the incentive, or even the inclination to reach out and bless others' lives if we ourselves have not first tasted and been transformed by the love of God. We love others sincerely and effectively when we allow our relationship with God to transform and impel our relationship with God's children. Elder Jeffrey R. Holland taught a profound truth when he declared that true charity has been known on this earth only once—as manifest in the grace and love and tender mercy extended to you and me through our Lord's atoning sacrifice.[1] Truly, "God so loved the world, that he gave his only begotten Son, that whosoever believeth in him should not perish, but have everlasting life" (John 3:16; compare D&C 34:3). We partake of the fruit of the tree of life as we exercise saving faith in Christ, repent of our sins, and dedicate ourselves to him and the cause of his gospel—in short, as we receive and appropriate the powers and gifts of the Atonement (1 Nephi 11:7, 21–22).

In speaking of the last days, Jesus said: "And in that day shall be heard of wars and rumors of wars, and the whole earth shall be in commotion, and *men's hearts shall fail them*, and they shall say that Christ delayeth his coming until the end of the earth. And *the love of men shall wax cold*, and *iniquity shall abound*" (D&C 45:26–27; emphasis added). Now consider the order of events as given in the Prophet Joseph's inspired translation of the twenty-fourth chapter of Matthew: "And again, *because iniquity shall abound, the love of men shall wax cold*; but he that shall not be overcome, the same shall be saved" (Joseph Smith–Matthew 1:30; emphasis added).

As wickedness widens, malevolence multiplies. As sin spreads, insensitivity intensifies. As immorality expands, the collective conscience shrinks and the sense of decency is deadened. The increase in our society of sarcasm, rudeness, crudeness, and hostility, child and spouse abuse, neglect of the innocent and the aged, and the continued death of the unborn through abortion—all these bespeak a gradual and too often unnoticed dehumanization, a definite desensitization. It is hauntingly significant that in the days of Noah "the earth was corrupt before God, and it was filled with violence. . . . And God said unto Noah: The end of all flesh is come before me, for the earth is filled with violence, and behold I will destroy all flesh from off the earth" (Moses 8:28, 30). It was not that long ago that two crazed fanatics planted bombs at the Boston Marathon, explosive devices that took human lives and maimed many others.

We are not, however, left without hope, nor need we surrender to the sadness of the sordid picture of what will be. We remember the Master's promise that "he that shall not be overcome, the same shall be saved" (Joseph Smith–Matthew 1:30). To the extent that the people of God keep themselves free from the sins of Sodom and Gomorrah, distance themselves from the unholy and the unclean, and sanctify themselves—separate themselves—from anything that defiles, degrades, and thus destroys the soul, they will not only save themselves but also preserve and protect their families and those they are charged to serve. To the extent that those who have received the fulness of the gospel honor their covenants, particularly those promises made in holy places, they will grow in spiritual power and stand as a stark contrast to the vain and pathetic heroes of the world.

We overcome the world as we become less interested in, less enamored of, and less ensnared by what the world and the worldly value. We overcome the world when we as disciples have developed that spiritual discipline, that "consciousness of victory over self" that opens the door to "communion with the Infinite" and thus to heightened spirituality.[2] We overcome the world as we determine that the one place where we would rather be than any other place on earth is our own home, as we seek to live in such a manner that we have the love and respect and confidence of our spouse and children, as we come to value that which is highly esteemed of holy beings and care little for the praise of the popular and the esteem of the enemies of God, and as we trust in and rely upon him who said, "In the world ye shall have tribulation: but be of good cheer; I have overcome the world" (John 16:33). We look to Christ to live and to live abundantly. The Prince of Peace brings solace to our souls and points us toward that marvelous millennial era when men and women will live in peace, when there will be "no contention in the land, because of the love of God which [dwells] in the hearts of the people" (4 Nephi 1:15). May God speed the right.

Chapter 4

FALSE CHRISTS

*M*any years ago a knock came at my office door. A young man (let's call him Ted) acknowledged that he was not currently a student of mine but asked if he might speak briefly with me. I learned that he had been reared in The Church of Jesus Christ of Latter-day Saints, that he was an Eagle Scout, had been enrolled in four years of seminary, had returned home from a full-time mission only months before, and was just beginning his course of study at Brigham Young University. He explained that his parents had been active, faithful members of the Church. In fact, his father had served for a time as a bishop.

His face clouded at this point, and his eyes filled with tears as he said, "Brother Millet, when I left for my mission, I left from a peaceful home and a family I was very proud of. But some things have gone wrong, terribly wrong." Ted then began to relate what proved to be an extremely painful story. He indicated that his parents, both in their forties, had reached that point in life after more than twenty years of marriage when they found that their lives had been so focused on the children—on Scouting and Young Women's camp and athletic contests and choirs and concerts and debates—that they realized they really had not devoted much of their energy to strengthening their marital relationship. They began to search for a marriage counselor or some kind of workshop that might help strengthen their union.

They happened upon a self-discovery class that was being held in the community, one advertised to be especially valuable for improving husband-wife relationships. At first, Ted recounted to me, everything seemed quite normal; during the first few weeks, participants in the class were taught how to focus more attention on the spouse, how to do active listening, and how to develop new interests in common. In addition, the instructor couched all that he discussed in class in terms of scriptural passages and prophetic statements. As the group moved into the second month of coursework, however, the spirit and mood of the activities began to change. The instructor became more animated, and the course of study became more intense. The class sessions began to be longer, sometimes stretching into the early morning hours. The young man reported that at this point his father began to be uneasy about some of the activities—strong verbal confrontations between marriage partners, holding hands with strangers, intimate conversations and time alone between persons who were not married to each other, repeated weekends away with the group, etc. As his father gradually stopped attending the class, his mother's involvement became even more pronounced. She went so far as to warn her husband that if he did not continue the course, she would divorce him. Ted said that he began to notice how his mother's countenance had changed, how devoted and loyal she became to the instructor and other classmates to the point that everything took a backseat to her new family, as she chose to call it.

Ted's father scheduled a time to meet with the bishop and related the sad tale. The bishop invited the mother in to meet with him, which she did. From what Ted could learn from his father, the bishop expressed his concerns with the kinds of unusual activities the self-discovery group encouraged and asked for the mother's reaction. She exploded and told the bishop, essentially, "You don't know what you're talking about. These sessions are deepening my spirituality and in general making me a more creative, sensitive, and caring person. This is the pure gospel. This is what Jesus would have all of us do. And if you can't live with that, then I don't need your church with its stifling standards and primitive moral codes." Within a short time, Ted's parents were divorced, and his mother moved in with the instructor. She no longer had any association with the family, and Ted and his siblings were left feeling emotionally beaten up and abused.

Ted and I spoke at some length about what he might do, since he now felt absolutely helpless. This is a true story but, unfortunately, not the only one of its kind I heard during my thirty years as a member of the Religious Education faculty at BYU. Several variations of this scenario were presented to me by distraught students who only wanted things in their home and family to be normal again. But they never were.

As he sat on the Mount of Olives with his disciples, only days before his crucifixion, Jesus delivered many of the signs of the times, prophecies of what would come to pass before his second coming in glory: "If any man shall say unto you, Lo, here is Christ, or there, believe him not; for *in those days there shall also arise false Christs,* and false prophets, and shall show great signs and wonders, insomuch, that, if possible, they shall deceive the very elect, who are the elect according to the covenant" (Joseph Smith–Matthew 1:21–22; emphasis added). Yes, I suppose there are a few deluded individuals who claim to be Jesus, or the reincarnated Jesus, or the feminine expression of Jesus (D&C 49).

There may be those who believe themselves to be messiahs, "anointed ones," savior figures who, having "read by the lamp of their own conceit,"[1] profess to be God's chosen vessels, called and elected to save us all from our naïve notions of reality. But in general, when the Lord warns of false Christs, he seems to be referring not so much to individuals as to tenets, teachings, and alternative pathways to happiness. "A false Christ is not a person," Elder Bruce R. McConkie explained. "It is a false system of worship, a false church, a false cult that says: 'Lo, here is salvation; here is the doctrine of Christ. Come and believe thus and so, and ye shall be saved.' It is any concept or philosophy that says that redemption, salvation, sanctification, justification, and all of the promised rewards can be gained in any way except that set forth by the apostles and prophets."[2]

In many ways, Ted's mother became enamored of a false Christ, that is, a social or behavioral system that holds out hope for fulfillment and spiritual wholeness in ways antithetical to the Lord's prescribed patterns for behavior and lifestyle. And of course there are false Christs to be found in individuals or institutions whose focus is economic or fraternal or philosophical. And yes, there are false Christs whose focus is political. These may attempt to proselytize us by an unhealthy and unstable allegiance to what they may call loyalty to the country through refusing to pay income taxes or by denouncing political parties other than their own. In time, the attitude of Latter-day Saints who have yielded themselves to this form of imbalance becomes one of, "Well, I know my politics are true, but I'm not so sure about my church." They begin to see and evaluate things through the lenses of their own gospel hobby. This is perilous.

From the scriptures of the Restoration we learn what might be called the principle of less than and more than. In his first visit to the Nephites, the risen Lord set forth what we know as the doctrine of Christ, the first principles and ordinances of the gospel. He then said: "Verily, verily, I say unto you, that this is my doctrine, and whoso buildeth upon this buildeth upon my rock, and the gates of hell shall not prevail against them. And *whoso shall declare more or less than this, and establish it for my doctrine, the same cometh of evil, and is not built upon my rock*; but he buildeth upon a sandy foundation, and the gates of hell stand open to receive such when the floods come and the winds beat upon them" (3 Nephi 11:39–40; emphasis added). In a revelation given in the summer of 1828, that same Lord again set forth the doctrine of Christ and added: "Whosoever repenteth and cometh unto me, the same is my church. *Whosoever declareth more or less than this, the same is not of me, but is against me*; therefore he is not of my church" (D&C 10:67–68; emphasis added; compare 93:24–25).

In the last days, the people of God must, absolutely must, stay in the mainstream of the Church—they must avoid any and all efforts to be truer than true, must take their cues from holy scripture as that scripture is interpreted and declared by living apostles and prophets, and must maintain and promote among those under their charge a sane and balanced approach to living. We are able to detect and reject from our lives those false Christs that arise in our day as we focus on fundamentals and delight in "declaring none other things than the prophets and apostles, that which they have seen and heard and most assuredly believe" (D&C 52:36). Therein is safety. Therein is peace.

Chapter 5
THE PRECEPTS OF MEN

$\mathcal{S}$everal years ago I had an experience that clearly illustrates the importance of staying doctrinally sound and following the Lord's pattern of authority. While I was serving as dean of Religious Education at Brigham Young University, the phone rang in my home early on a Saturday morning. My wife, Shauna, answered and a few seconds later handed me the receiver. "It's for you."

The caller was an apostle and a member of the board of trustees of BYU. He had my full attention.

Getting right to the point, he asked, "Bob, are you aware of the book [by a member of the Church] that is so popular these days?" The book had been released through a national publishing house; it had by that time become a national best-seller.

I responded, "Yes, I am aware of it. A few weeks ago I bought it and have since read it."

"What do you think about it?" he asked.

I commented hesitantly that I had some doctrinal concerns about several of the main points made by the author.

"I would hope so!" he said. He asked what my concerns were, and I spelled them out. "Yes, those are some of the things that bothered me, as well," he replied.

Then there was a slight pause and silence. What followed are words that I will never forget, frightening words from an apostle of the Lord Jesus Christ: "Sometimes our lack of doctrinal sophistication makes us easy prey to such fads."

Soberly, I voiced my concurrence.

Jesus warned not only of false Christs but also of false prophets (Matthew 7:15; Joseph Smith–Matthew 1:22). I suppose that false prophets could take many forms, but essentially they all are individuals who claim to speak for God but have not received the requisite divine authorization. A modern revelation offers this warning: "Behold, I am from above, and my power lieth beneath. I am over all, and in all, and through all, and search all things, and the day cometh that all things shall be subject unto me. Behold, I am Alpha and Omega, even Jesus Christ. Wherefore, let all men beware how they take my name in their lips—for behold, verily I say, that *many there be who are under this condemnation, who use the name of the Lord, and use it in vain, having not authority*" (D&C 63:59–62; emphasis added).

False prophets spread false precepts. In speaking of the era of the Restoration, the Lord observed that "when the times of the Gentiles is come in," the time in which we now live, when the gospel has been restored to a culturally Gentile people (see D&C 109:60), a "light shall break forth among them that sit in darkness, and it shall be the fulness of my gospel; but they receive it not; for they perceive not the light, and they turn their hearts from me because of the precepts of men" (D&C 45:28–29). This passage reminds me of the words of Nephi, son of Lehi, who spoke prophetically of the last days: "They have all gone astray save it be a few, who are the humble followers of Christ; nevertheless, . . . *they* [the humble followers of Christ] *do err because they are taught by the precepts of men*" (2 Nephi 28:14; emphasis added).

Every so often someone rises up and claims some special knowledge, some saving authority, some crucial revelation from God. How can we know? How shall we distinguish between that which is of God and that which is from either man or the devil? (D&C 46:7). There are ways of knowing the truth, of discerning the veracity and fruitfulness of a doctrine or point of view. Joseph Smith pointed out that "nothing is a greater injury to the children of men than to be under the influence of a false spirit when they think they have the Spirit of God."[1] If someone comes to us claiming a special appointment, special knowledge that is not available to most members, special training and abilities that entitle him or her to interpret scripture or clarify doctrine beyond what has been given by the authorized servants of God, we might ask the following questions:

1. *Is the person claiming a divine communication or insight acting within the bounds of his or her respective assignment?* The Lord's house is a house of order, not a house of confusion (D&C 132:8). Chaos would ensue quickly if every person could receive revelations for every other person in the Church, irrespective of stewardship. Joseph Smith the Prophet taught that "it is contrary to the economy of God for any member of the Church, or any one, to receive instructions for those in authority, higher than themselves."[2] He also explained that it is the "privilege of any officer in this Church to obtain revelations, so far as relates to his particular calling and duty in the Church."[3] Through the generations people have repeatedly insisted that they have received direction for the Church regarding its financial status, its placement of temples, its meetings or schedule, and its doctrinal positions on this or that topic. No matter the genuineness or sincerity of the supposed recipients, the directives are not of God. The Lord simply does not work that way. There is order. There are proper channels.

2. *Is the recipient of the communication worthy to receive it?* We may not always be in a position to judge another's worthiness, but we are generally pretty good judges of our own. The revelations indicate that the works of God are brought to pass through those who are clean, who have been purified from the sins of the world (3 Nephi 8:1; D&C 50:28). If I have received what I believe to be a revelation from God, then it is perfectly appropriate for me to ask myself (and it would be well if I asked with sincerity and humility) whether I was in spiritual condition to receive such a communication from God. There is a great lesson to be learned from the Savior's Last Supper. After Jesus announced to the Twelve that one of them would betray him, we do not read of the apostles saying such things as "I know who it is. It's Judas. He's been acting strange for some time now." Instead, they responded, "Lord, is it I?" (Matthew 26:22).

3. *Is the communication in harmony with the teachings in the standard works and those of the living prophets?* When people claim to have received word that they should join a polygamous cult or participate in a demonic practice or be disloyal or disobedient to the government, one wonders how they can justify their position. When others indicate that they have been directed by the Lord to lie or cheat or steal or be immoral, one wonders how such actions can be squared with the teachings of the Church. Often individuals claim that their case is an exception to the rule. We would do well as a people to stay within the rules and avoid the exceptions, especially when such exceptions violate the laws and the order of the kingdom of God. Those still convinced that what they are commanded to do is of God would then do well to counsel with their priesthood leaders and then follow that counsel diligently. On the other hand, certain groups of people contend that the Church should be doing this or that to be in harmony with such

and such a scripture. We need only remind ourselves that ours is a living church, with a living constitution (D&C 1:30), and that the principle on which the government of heaven is conducted is, as Joseph Smith stated, "revelation adapted to the circumstances in which the children of the kingdom are placed."[4] Wise counsel for the Saints was given by Elder Bruce R. McConkie when he said: "The proper course for all of us is to stay in the mainstream of the Church. This is the Lord's Church, and it is led by the spirit of inspiration, and the practice of the Church constitutes the interpretation of the scripture."[5]

4. *Does the communication edify or instruct? Is it consistent with the dignity that should attend something that comes from the Almighty?* The Prophet taught that God's revelations communicate something of worth to us. He also pointed out that a certain dignity and decorum are associated with divine communications.[6]

5. *Does the communication build our faith and strengthen our commitment?* There is a litmus test that can be applied, a vital criterion that must be met if a supposed revelation is from God. We ask such questions as the following: Does this communication build my faith in Joseph Smith and the Restoration? Do I feel more motivated to serve faithfully in the Church and kingdom? Does it buttress my confidence in the Lord's anointed servants today and in the destiny of the Church? God does not and will not work against himself; he will not confuse his people by having them believe or do things that would in any way weaken their hold on the iron rod. Those who suggest that the present Church is not progressive enough, that it needs to move faster toward this or that social or political or moral end, act outside the bounds of propriety. They are walking on slippery ground. Joseph Smith stated: "That man who rises up to condemn others, finding fault with the Church, saying that they are out of the way, while he himself is righteous,

then know assuredly, that that man is in the high road to apostasy; and if he does not repent, will apostatize, as God lives."[7]

Jesus taught that prophets are known by their fruits (Matthew 7:16, 20), that is, by what their word brings forth, the product of their proclamations. How does it affect individuals and families? To what extent does it encourage unity and harmony, wholeness and well-being? God be praised that we live in a day and time when apostles and prophets walk the earth! The fulness of the gospel of Jesus Christ has been restored to the earth, and there will never again be an apostasy of the Lord's Church. "How long are they [the prophets] to remain in the Church? 'Till we all come in the unity of the faith'; until that millennial day when every living soul is converted to the truth; until righteous men are prepared to receive their own instructions direct from the Lord."[8]

The Saints of the Most High need not become prey to false prophets, to false precepts, to spurious revelations. We have the gift of the Holy Ghost, and we are duty bound to seek those spiritual gifts that enable us to choose wisely and avoid deception (D&C 46:8). As we hearken to the counsel of those we sustain as prophets, seers, and revelators we walk firmly on gospel sod. We insulate ourselves against false and corrupting teachings.

Chapter 6

"GO YE OUT FROM BABYLON"

*J*ust as putting on Christ (Romans 13:14) always entails putting off the natural man (Ephesians 4:22; Colossians 3:8–9; Mosiah 3:19), even so establishing a foothold in Zion always requires that we leave Babylon behind. How frequently Jehovah has called upon his people: "Depart ye, depart ye, go ye out from thence, touch no unclean thing; go ye out of the midst of her; be ye clean, that bear the vessels of the Lord" (Isaiah 52:11). In our dispensation that clarion call has been sounded again. Those who aspire to holiness are told to "sanctify yourselves. . . . Go ye out from Babylon. Be ye clean that bear the vessels of the Lord" (D&C 133:4–5).

In speaking of the scriptural phrase "Be ye clean, that bear the vessels of the Lord," Elder Jeffrey R. Holland offered valuable instruction to the holders of the Aaronic and Melchizedek Priesthoods: "Anciently it had at least two meanings, both related to the work of the priesthood.

"The first refers to the recovery and return to Jerusalem of various temple implements that had been carried into Babylon by King Nebuchadnezzar. In physically handling the return of these items, the Lord reminded those early brethren of the sanctity of anything related to the temple. Therefore as they carried back to their homeland these various bowls, basins, cups, and other vessels, they themselves were to be as clean as the ceremonial instruments they bore.

"The second meaning is related to the first. Similar bowls and implements were used for ritual purification in the home. The Apostle Paul, writing to his young friend Timothy, said of these, 'In a great house there are . . . vessels of gold and . . . silver, . . . of wood and of earth'—these means of washing and cleansing common in the time of the Savior. But Paul goes on to say, 'If a man . . . purge himself [of unworthiness], *he* shall *be* a vessel . . . sanctified, and meet for the master's use, and prepared unto every good work.' Therefore, Paul says, 'Flee . . . youthful lusts: . . . follow righteousness, . . . call on the Lord out of a pure heart.' [2 Timothy 2:20–22; emphasis added]."[1]

We go out from Babylon when we consciously choose to remove ourselves from and avoid people and places and circumstances that have in the past proven to be compromising and costly; when we consciously choose to walk forward on the path of truth and righteousness, never looking back on the life or deeds or associations we have left behind (Genesis 19:17); when we consciously choose to take our spiritual cues and establish our moral values from holy scripture and living prophets, forsaking the fads and formulas of television or Hollywood personalities who beckon to us from the great and spacious building; when we consciously choose to stand regularly and more consistently in holy places; and when we consciously choose to cast our vote for the Lord's Church, so that our soul cry becomes, "The kingdom of God or nothing!" "Faith," as Elder Neil L. Andersen pointed out, "is not only a feeling; it is a decision."[2]

As members of the restored Church, we are striving to

become *holy*. Webster's 1828 *Dictionary* states, "We call a man holy, when his heart is conformed in some degree to the image of God, and his life is regulated by the divine precepts."[3] A holy person is therefore one who lives a life that is patterned after the Savior's, in which divine precepts both motivate and monitor one's conduct. We live in a day that militates against holiness, when time-honored values are ridiculed, and when those who stand up for morality are marginalized in society. It is, in fact, the day of Satan's power, in which evil is called good and good is called evil, in which darkness is labeled light and light is labeled darkness (Isaiah 5:20; 2 Nephi 15:20). Because society's slouch toward Gomorrah will persist, it is increasingly difficult to ascertain moral truth in the world and dangerous to follow current and future trends.[4] We take our cues from society at our peril.

Too many things an earlier generation would have spurned and rejected as deadly to their souls have been allowed to become part of our world. Some of this has happened as a result of excessive tolerance or misplaced loyalty. Let me illustrate. A few years ago a student at Brigham Young University asked to visit with me after class. She had been a student of mine for two semesters of Book of Mormon, and she was, frankly, a delight to have in class. The light of the gospel radiated from her countenance. She came in to tell me good-bye. I said, "I'll see you next year, won't I?"

She shook her head. "No, I won't be coming back to BYU." When I asked why, she said, "Brother Millet, I'm tired. No, it's more than that—I'm worn out. I haven't slept for almost a year now." Was she tired of studying? I asked. Wouldn't a summer break do the trick? No, that wasn't it. She explained that her roommates, all returned missionaries, had their boyfriends over each night until the early morning hours. I was stunned. "Why haven't you told someone? Why didn't you mention it to the landlord or the bishop?" Her answer highlights a significant problem that many in this generation face. She said, "But wouldn't that be judging them?" We had a lengthy discussion about what it meant to judge righteous judgment (JST, Matthew 7:1–2; John 7:24). I explained to her that each of us, as men and women seeking to be holy, are under obligation to make judgments every day of our lives. We must decide whether we will spend time with certain people, in certain places, doing certain things. Such decisions, very much a part of making our way through the mists of darkness, are vital; our hope for eternal life depends upon our doing so.[5] My young friend had, in the words of President Boyd K. Packer, fallen into the "tolerance trap."[6]

Too many among us try to live on the edge, to play percentages with God, to tempt fate, and to place themselves in circumstances that can contribute to their spiritual undoing. There are those who want to see how far they can go without going all the way, those who want to drive as close to the edge of the cliff as possible without falling, those who cunningly creep up on the flame with no intention of being burned, those who want to enjoy all the allurements of Babylon but at the same time retain their citizenship in Zion.

There is no lasting happiness in such approaches to life but rather a type of moral or spiritual schizophrenia. Too many people want to be good—but not too good; others want to be bad—but not too bad. Some want to serve the Lord without offending the devil. As my colleague Brent Top once observed, one cannot dance in the great and spacious building and still hold onto the iron rod; clinging to the iron rod requires both hands, as well as heart and soul. James taught that "a double minded man is unstable in all his ways" (James 1:8). We would do well to stay as far away from sin and compromise as we can, not only to avoid evil but also to avoid the very appearance of evil (1 Thessalonians 5:22). Prevention is far, far better than extrication.

President George Albert Smith taught: "There are two influences in the world today, and have been from the beginning. One is an influence that is constructive, that radiates happiness and builds character. The other influence is one that destroys, turns men into demons, tears down and discourages. We are all susceptible to both. The one comes from our Heavenly Father, and the other comes from the source of evil that has been in the world from the beginning, seeking to bring about the destruction of the human family. . . .

"My grandfather used to say to his family, 'There is a line of demarkation, well defined, between the Lord's territory and the devil's. If you will stay on the Lord's side of the line you will be under his influence and will have no desire to do wrong; but if you cross to the devil's side of the line one inch, you are in the tempter's power, and if he is successful, you will not be able to think or even reason properly, because you will have lost the spirit of the Lord.'

"When I have been tempted sometimes to do a certain thing, I have asked myself, 'Which side of the line am I on?' If I determined to be on the safe side, the Lord's side, I would do the right thing every time. So when temptation comes, think prayerfully about your problem, and the influence of the spirit of the Lord will enable you to decide wisely. There is safety for us only on the Lord's side of the line."[7]

We can put away the things of this world and become a people of purpose. We can begin to change society, one person at a time. We have the promise that "they that be with us are more than they that be with them" (2 Kings 6:16), that, as John the Beloved instructed the Saints in his day, "Greater is he that is in you, than he that is in the world" (1 John 4:4). The charge and the promise given to the ancient Israelites by Joshua is remarkably pertinent in our day: "Sanctify yourselves: for to morrow the Lord will do wonders among you" (Joshua 3:5). God grant that we, the people of the everlasting covenant, will be wise in the days of our probation, that we will put away the foolishness of the flesh and put out of our lives those things that have no place among a people concerned with the establishment of Zion.

Chapter 7
OUR LAMPS FILLED WITH OIL

Years ago I sat opposite a husband and wife who had come to visit their bishop in a time of crisis. "We need help, Bishop Millet. Our family is falling apart, our marriage is on the rocks, and the children, now in their late teens, are eager to get out of the home as soon as possible." This family was one we often refer to as less active, although that description is generous in their case; so far as I could determine, these people, although their names were certainly on the records of the Church, had not attended Church meetings or participated in any way for many, many years. The husband added, "The two of us have decided that what we need most is spirituality in our home. Could you please help us, Bishop?"

We visited about the kinds of things that invite the Spirit of the Lord into our lives, and I made specific suggestions. "Why not begin with a regular and consistent study of the scriptures, both as individuals and as a family?"

The husband (let's call him Fred) responded, "I hate to read. Besides, reading hurts my eyes. There must be something else we could do."

I swallowed and tried again. "Well, okay, what about beginning to have family prayer in the morning and at night."

Immediately the wife (let's call her Helen) reacted. "But our family goes in so many directions in the morning and at night that it's impossible to get us together just to talk to one another, much less to God."

I tried again. "Well, then, why don't we talk for a few minutes about how to hold an effective family home evening once each week?"

Fred blurted out, "Isn't that supposed to be on Monday nights? I bowl every Monday night, and Helen's bridge game is the same night."

In a last-ditch effort, I said, "It sounds like your week is packed with activities. Can we count on you to be at church this Sunday? Sacrament meeting, the main worship service, is at 9:00, followed by Sunday School and then priesthood and Relief Society." Helen and Fred stared at each other for about thirty seconds and then looked reluctantly back at me. Helen said, "Bishop, both of us work pretty long hours six days a week. Sunday is the one day we can take it easy, the one segment of time when we can kick back and relax."

I sat behind my desk feeling both dumbfounded and frustrated. I sighed in a way that was intended to be heard and said, "Okay, let's start over. Helen and Fred, what can I do to help you? What is it that you need?"

Without hesitation, Fred reiterated, "It's like I mentioned earlier. We simply need to get more of God's Spirit in our home!"

It was as if this couple were pleading with me, "Bishop, could you please reach into your mind, pull out the results of years of scripture study, and give them to us? While you're at it, perhaps we could have some of your lifetime of personal and family prayer, decades of family home evening, and the sweet blessings that flow into our lives from being in attendance at thousands of Church worship services."

It was on this occasion, and I remember it distinctly, that I finally began to grasp some of the profound messages of the parable of the ten virgins. To be honest, that parable had bothered me for a long time. My attitude was essentially, "Why can't the wise virgins just break down and share some of their oil with the foolish ones? Didn't Jesus teach them to share?"

I looked at Fred and Helen and felt much love and compassion for them but also a great deal of sorrow, for I realized that there are some things that simply can't be shared. I can share my testimony with another person of the reality of God, the saving efficacy of the blood of Jesus Christ, and the truthfulness of the restored gospel. I can share insights into a scriptural passage or express my delight in an inspirational message from a modern prophet. I can share with a man or woman who is searching for peace and deliverance from the ignorance and agnosticism of our day just what a difference the plan of salvation provides—sweet and stimulating perspective into where we came from, why we are here on earth, and where we will go when we leave mortality. But some things cannot be borrowed or lent.

Elder David A. Bednar asked: "Were the five wise virgins selfish and unwilling to share, or were they indicating correctly that the oil of conversion cannot be borrowed? Can the spiritual strength that results from consistent obedience to the commandments be given to another person? Can the knowledge obtained through diligent study and pondering of the scriptures be conveyed to one who is in need? Can the peace the gospel brings to a faithful Latter-day Saint be transferred to an individual experiencing adversity or great challenge? The clear answer to each of these questions is no.

"As the wise virgins emphasized properly, each of us must 'buy for ourselves.' These inspired women were not describing a business transaction; rather, they were emphasizing our individual responsibility to keep our lamp of testimony burning and to obtain an ample supply of the oil of conversion. This precious oil is acquired one drop at a time—'line upon line [and] precept upon precept' (2 Nephi 28:30), patiently and persistently. No shortcut is available; no last-minute flurry of preparation is possible."[1]

The Son of Man has spoken: "And at that day, when I shall come in my glory, shall the parable be fulfilled which I spake concerning the ten virgins. For *they that are wise and have received the truth, and have taken the Holy Spirit for their guide,* and have not been deceived—verily I say unto you, they shall not be hewn down and cast into the fire, but shall abide the day" (D&C 45:56–57; emphasis added). And so the faithful, like the wise virgins in the parable, are those who "have received the truth, and have taken the Holy Spirit for their guide." They are wise in that they strive to grasp the principles and precepts of holy scripture and delight in the contemporary counsel of those special men who see things not visible to the natural eye (Moses 6:36), who see not only the distant road but also the challenges that await us around the corners of life. And they are wise in that they take the Holy Spirit for their guide.

One crucial decision we must make as followers of the Christ is where we will turn for direction and to which of the competing voices in the world we will attend. To whom shall we listen? Whom shall we follow? We can turn to scripture, particularly the New Testament and the Book of Mormon, to learn how Jesus taught, how he talked, how he was fearless in confronting evil, how he ministered one-by-one to those who were lonely or in pain and distress, how dependent upon and submissive to his Heavenly Father he was, and how his eye was single to the glory of God from the cradle to the cross. But how would we ever know what Jesus would do in a business venture, in a family crisis, in deep financial woes? How would Jesus handle dilemmas that you and I face in the twenty-first century? What *would* Jesus do? It is not always possible to emulate the Savior by merely turning to specific scriptural episodes; as powerful as the Gospels are, we cannot always find Jesus in identical situations with our own. There is no way that every eventuality could be chronicled in scripture, and so we must turn elsewhere.

Shall we turn to the Church and its auxiliaries? To the handbooks and manuals for specific guidance? Of course, but here again we will eventually be frustrated. Why? Because even the Lord's Church and its leaders cannot dot every 'i' and cross every 't' for us. The Church of Jesus Christ will teach us timely and timeless principles, but it is to the Holy Ghost that we must turn for specific practices. It is not uncommon to hear Latter-day Saints ask in earnestness, "What comes first, the Church or the family? The family or the Church? What should be my highest priority?" In fact, it is the Lord God who must come first in our lives, and the Spirit will whisper what should come second in each instance.

We have been counseled to "be faithful, praying always, having your lamps trimmed and burning, and oil with you, that you may be ready at the coming of the Bridegroom" (D&C 33:17). We seek to acquire the oil that brings light into our lives, a light that conveys not only information but also perspective.

The people of King Benjamin were deeply and permanently changed by his profound message to them. They believed his

words, knew by revelation that his teachings were true, and acknowledged that they had undergone a mighty change, such that
they had "no more disposition to do evil, but to do good continually." Now notice what follows, a verse we seldom discuss: "And
we, ourselves, also, through the infinite goodness of God, and
the manifestations of his Spirit, have great views of that which is
to come; and were it expedient, we could prophesy of all things"
(Mosiah 5:2–3; emphasis added). Great views, indeed! It is by
and through the work of the Spirit of the Living God upon our
minds and hearts that we understand things now and prepare for
that which is yet to be.

We seek to acquire the oil that is a healing balm, a mighty
medicine for the wounds we bear from the spears and arrows that
strike us in the midst of the battle for the souls of individuals.
It is by the power of the Comforter, who "knoweth all things"
(D&C 42:17), that loneliness and alienation, embarrassment
and feelings of inadequacy, abuse and neglect, jealousy and fear
are overcome. It is through the quiet curative we know as the
Spirit that we are able to have bitterness and anger removed
from our hearts, to have sin and self-obsession and arrogance
burned out of our souls as though by fire. For that third member
of the Godhead, the one referred to by the Lord Jesus as "another Comforter" (John 14:16; D&C 88:3), is also the Sanctifier,
the One sent by the Father as the spiritual midwife of the new
birth, the One tasked with purifying and transforming our minds
(Romans 12:1–2), the One who enables the Saints of God to
gain "the mind of Christ" (1 Corinthians 2:16).

Not one of us wants to walk the paths of this life in doubt
about our spiritual standing before God, ever wondering what
is good enough and when enough is truly enough. No amount
of study, even the study of holy scripture, can bring to us this

supernal understanding, can allow us to know that we are walking in paths of righteousness and that our course in life is pleasing to that God who is also our Father in heaven.[2] Such knowledge can come to us only as the Holy Spirit of Promise, who is the Holy Ghost, or the Holy Spirit promised to the Saints, causes to distil upon us what the apostle Paul called the "earnest of the Spirit in our hearts" or the "earnest of our inheritance" (2 Corinthians 1:22; Ephesians 1:13–14). In a very real way, God's "earnest money" on us, his token or promise that he seriously intends to save and exalt us, is the Holy Ghost. When the Spirit is with us, it is a sign from God that we are on course, a candidate for eternal glory, headed for the celestial kingdom, worthy of "peace in this world, and eternal life in the world to come" (D&C 59:23). It is the "helmet of salvation" (Ephesians 6:17) worn by the Christian soldier and, more specifically, the "helmet [of] *the hope of salvation*" (1 Thessalonians 5:8; emphasis added).

That is to say, if you and I continue faithful to our covenants, the day will come when God will seal the anointing that we have received and give us entrance, with our families, into his eternal presence. This is no doubt what Benjamin meant when he encouraged his people to "be steadfast and immovable, always abounding in good works, *that Christ, the Lord God Omnipotent, may seal you his, that you may be brought to heaven, that ye may have everlasting salvation and eternal life*, through the wisdom, and power, and justice, and mercy of him who created all things, in heaven and in earth, who is God above all" (Mosiah 5:15; emphasis added).

President Jedediah M. Grant, who served as a counselor to President Brigham Young in the First Presidency, pointed out: "Many in the world would suppose that when they preach and circulate the Bible, they actually put in the possession of the people that power and life and those gifts, that the ancient Apostles and Prophets and Saints of God enjoyed.

"Brethren and sisters, we understand the difference between enjoying and reading of enjoyment, between the history of a feast and the feast itself; also between the history of the law of God and the law itself.

"When the Prophet Joseph came among the people he did not tell them that he would sell them the word of God, but after he had established the truth in their minds and they were baptized, he then laid his hands upon them that they might receive the gift of the Holy Ghost, for he had promised this, and they received the Holy Comforter and the same light, the same Spirit, the same power of God, and the same principles of eternal life; *that very gift which is the greatest gift of God, and it gave them the same joy, and the same great blessings, and this Spirit taught them the will of God.*"[3]

We cannot, at least not for very long, operate simply by sheer grit and willpower; to do so proves to be both spiritually exhausting and emotionally discouraging. We need help. That help comes to us from God and is mediated through his Holy Spirit. It just may be that the most significant and enduring effort in which we as members of the Lord's Church can choose to be involved, the most elevated and enriching endeavor we may undertake, is to live in such a manner that the Spirit of the Lord can be, as promised, our constant companion. That is the oil brought by the wise virgins, the oil that must fill the lamps of those men and women of destiny who are now preparing the world for the coming of the Bridegroom. It is the means by which comfort, perspective, and spiritual drive come to us, and the avenue through which we enjoy God's holy comfort.

Chapter 8

TREASURING UP THE WORD

*A*fter reciting many of the signs incident to his coming in glory—false Christs, false prophets, wars and rumors of wars, the gathering of the Saints, famines, pestilences, and earthquakes, the spread of the message of salvation to every nation and tongue, and unusual signs in the heavens—the Savior added this priceless promise: "And whoso treasureth up my word, shall not be deceived" (Joseph Smith–Matthew 1:37). What marvelous counsel! We avoid deception through treasuring up the word of God.

And how do we do that? Most of us have a sense for what a treasure is, but what does it mean when we change this word into a verb, or action word, as to *treasure* something? Obviously, it means to treat it as precious, to prize, to cherish, to value greatly, to hold in high esteem. In a revelation given through the Prophet Joseph Smith in February 1831, the Lord, after having spoken of our need to prepare for his second coming and the great millennial day, added: "Hearken ye to these words. Behold, I am Jesus Christ, the Savior of the world. *Treasure these things up in your hearts, and let the solemnities of eternity rest upon your minds.* Be sober. Keep all my commandments" (D&C 43:34–35; emphasis added).

While life is meant to be enjoyed and our associations and

encounters with others are sometimes pleasurable, the disciples of Christ also recognize that there are some things that must be taken seriously, some matters of sublime import that are deserving of deep and sober reflection. Amulek explained that "this life is the time for men to prepare to meet God." He declared that we must never "procrastinate the day of [our] repentance until the end; for after this day of life, which is given us to prepare for eternity, behold, if we do not improve our time"—that is, make wise and careful use of it—"while in this life, then cometh the night of darkness wherein there can be no labor performed" (Alma 34:32–33). Because we are largely a product of what occupies our minds and because our feelings and actions are so inextricably linked to our thoughts, we must see to it that what we think about is worthy of a son or daughter of God striving for exaltation in the celestial kingdom. Frankly, eternity is a solemn matter. How we will spend eternity and who we will spend it with are solemn matters. We ignore them or refuse to think of them at our spiritual peril.

How in the world can we prepare for life in the highest heaven if indeed our thoughts are dominated by the lowest elements in our society? Now, to be sure, we do not expect to hold communion with angels every minute, nor are most of us privileged to be able to think about the scriptures or talk about the prophetic word a great deal during the working day. But I have met many a person who has chosen to spend a few moments away from the job, perhaps at lunch, to read for enlightenment or to pray for a greater measure of strength. I have become acquainted with noble souls who use their driving-home time to listen to general conference addresses or uplifting music. And I have been thrilled to encounter Latter-day Saints who have become engaged in what has, sadly, become almost a lost art—the memorization and recitation of the scriptures and words of modern prophets. Isn't this what Christ had in mind when he counseled the early Saints to "treasure up in your minds continually the words of life"? (D&C 84:85). Truly, you and I will become what we think about.

Let me share a few of my own feelings about scripture memorization. This was something I did for the first time as a full-time missionary. The more than three hundred scriptures I committed to memory between 1967 and 1969 have proven to be foundational to my study of the doctrines and principles of the restored gospel and my deep love for them. I find myself still, in the middle of talks or lessons, drawing upon passages I memorized more than forty years ago. Recently I decided to do what I had been wanting to do for some time—to commit to memory some of my favorite scriptural passages and words of the Prophet Joseph Smith that I have paraphrased for decades. I wanted to memorize, for example, Doctrine and Covenants 11:12; 81:5; 103:36; 108:7; and 121:33–46, as well as Brother Joseph's powerful words that "the Standard of Truth has been erected" in the Wentworth Letter,[1] which many missionaries since my time have committed to memory. The other beloved expression by Joseph Smith that I wanted in my head and heart is as follows: "It is my meditation all the day, and more than my meat and drink, to know how I shall make the Saints of God comprehend the visions that roll like an overflowing surge before my mind."[2]

I must admit that memorizing was a tougher exercise at sixty-five than it was at nineteen and twenty. But now, several times a week, usually after personal study, I recite aloud those scriptures and wonderful statements of the Prophet. In doing so I am lifted and encouraged; my faith and conviction are strengthened. And it takes me about five minutes. There is power in this endeavor, supernal power, and I feel it profoundly as I treasure aloud those sacred words. Elder Richard G. Scott pointed out:

"Because scriptures are generated from inspired communication through the Holy Ghost, they are pure truth. We need not be concerned about the validity of concepts contained in the standard works since the Holy Ghost has been the instrument which has motivated and inspired those individuals who have recorded the scriptures.

"Scriptures are like packets of light that illuminate our minds and give place to guidance and inspiration from on high. They can become the key to open the channel to communion with our Father in Heaven and His Beloved Son, Jesus Christ.

"The scriptures provide the strength of authority to our declarations when they are cited correctly. They can become stalwart friends that are not limited by geography or calendar. They are always available when needed. Their use provides a foundation of truth that can be awakened by the Holy Ghost. Learning, pondering, searching, and memorizing scriptures is like filling a filing cabinet with friends, values, and truths that can be called upon anytime, anywhere in the world.

"Great power can come from memorizing scriptures. To memorize a scripture is to forge a new friendship. It is like discovering a new individual who can help in time of need, give inspiration and comfort, and be a source of motivation for needed change."[3]

To treasure, then, is also to retain carefully, to store up, to put away for a later time when it might be needed. To use a scriptural phrase, when we treasure the word of the Lord, we "lay up in store" sacred matters (D&C 4:4); we put them in savings or invest them for later use. Through this means, on subsequent occasions and perhaps at a time of great spiritual need, the Comforter can "teach [us] all things, and bring all things to [our] remembrance" that we have read or studied or memorized previously (John 14:26). In his marvelous Sermon on the Mount, the Savior instructed his disciples that "where your treasure is, there will your heart be also" (Matthew 6:21). Indeed, that which we treasure is dear to our hearts, precious to our souls, eternal in its consequences. As the sincere followers of the Savior treasure his word, they ready themselves to become pillars in the temple of our God (Revelation 3:12), rich resources to the children of our Father in heaven, solid and significant stalwarts in the faith.

Chapter 9
STANDING IN HOLY PLACES

In the Bible, the earliest mortal episode of human interaction with the divine is that of the creation, placement on earth, and fall of Adam and Eve. Satan came into the garden and tempted Eve. She yielded to his enticements and partook of the forbidden fruit, which she then shared with Adam. God appeared, our first parents confessed their misdeed, and they were cast from the Garden of Eden to till the earth and make their way by the sweat of their brow. The Prophet Joseph's inspired translation of this episode, as we find it in the book of Moses, adds the marvelous perspective that enables us to understand this series of events not as the first human tragedy, not as the initial act of human rebellion, not as a selfish effort to usurp divine powers but rather as a fortunate fall, a significant part of the plan of God. In the words of Elder Orson F. Whitney, the Fall "had a twofold direction—downward, yet forward. It brought man into the world and set his feet upon progression's highway."[1] The Fall opened the door to mortality, which resulted in sin and death, but also laid the foundation for a redemption and a reconciliation that would come in and through the atonement and resurrection of Jesus

Christ. Truly, as C. S. Lewis wrote, "redeemed humanity" would rise higher, infinitely higher, than "unfallen humanity."[2]

In describing Adam and Eve's interaction with God, Genesis records that they "heard the voice of the Lord God walking in the garden in the cool of the day: and Adam and his wife hid themselves from the presence of the Lord God amongst the trees of the garden." Then follows this most fascinating sentence: "And the Lord God called unto Adam, and said unto him, *Where art thou?*" (Genesis 3:8–9; emphasis added). As we might suppose, this question has given rise to much conversation and commentary through the centuries, the essence of which is a question like this: Why would an all-wise, all-knowing Being need to ask Adam where he was? Couldn't God find him? Is it possible that Adam and Eve could escape to some corner of the globe where the Almighty would be unable to discern their whereabouts? Hardly, for the scriptures attest that there is no place humans can go that God cannot find them and find them out. No, God knew perfectly well where Adam and Eve were, but perhaps Adam and Eve needed to know where they were.

"Where art thou?" God asks each of us regularly, through his Spirit, through the holy scriptures, through the words of living oracles. Dennis Rasmussen, professor emeritus of philosophy at Brigham Young University, wrote: "Man's fundamental need is not to ask a question but to respond to one. Only by responding do I learn to be responsible; only by responding do I learn to care about something beyond myself.

" . . . When Adam left Eden, the Lord clothed his body with a garment and his soul with a question. Adam, where art thou? *Does God not know? On the contrary, only he knows. In my weakness I lose my bearings.* Like a child wandering in a forest I follow the whims of the moment and forget the way. I am too caught up by my surroundings to follow the path. *Not until a Father's voice calls do I wonder where I am.* How shall I answer? I am here? But where is here? So helpless am I that I cannot say. But deep within I hear his voice and tremble, for finally there are just two places, with him or without him, and just two ways, toward him or not toward him."[3]

The great question as rendered in Joseph Smith's translation of the Bible is slightly different: "And I, the Lord God, called unto Adam, and said unto him: *Where goest thou?*" (Moses 4:15; emphasis added). That is, essentially, "Adam, where are you headed? Eve, what's your destination?" It is extremely valuable, in the midst of today's maddeningly fast-paced world, to stop for a moment, take a breath, reflect, and reorient oneself. No one of us lives without sin, and every one of us is in need of pardoning mercy. We stray, and then we strive to get back on course. We are pained when we step momentarily out of the light but encouraged when we read the precious words of the Lord that "as often as my people repent will I forgive them their trespasses against me" (Mosiah 26:30).

A modern revelation contains these sobering words: "And there shall be men standing in that generation"—the generation "in which [the signs of the times] shall be shown forth" (Joseph Smith–Matthew 1:34)—"that shall not pass until they see an overflowing scourge; for a desolating sickness shall cover the land. But *my disciples shall stand in holy places,* and shall not be moved" (D&C 45:31–32; emphasis added). Note the message in another place: "Behold, it is my will, that all they who call on my name, and worship me according to mine everlasting gospel, should gather together, and stand in holy places" (D&C 101:22). From the beginning, Jehovah has sought to establish "a chosen generation, a royal priesthood, an holy nation, a peculiar

STANDING IN HOLY PLACES ✎ 49

people" (1 Peter 2:9; compare Exodus 19:5). A holy nation consists of those who have learned to stand in holy places. Yes, those
who seek earnestly to follow the Savior must always be found in
Church buildings and in holy temples; these are the houses of the
Lord. We prepare to dwell with him forever in the life to come by
spending in this life a significant portion of our time in his abode.

The crucial issue, however, is not our specific geography. No,
it is not *where* we are so much as *how* we are; as we have been
taught, our standing before God is less about what we are doing
than about what we are *becoming*.[4] We stand in holy places when
we let it be known that we are Latter-day Saints and that we
have something of transcendent value to offer the world; when
we dare to be different; when we stand up for the right; when
we endure the crosses of the world and despise the shame of it
(2 Nephi 9:18); when we care little for the fads and fashions of
the culture and determine to be a part of Zion's counterculture.
We stand in holy places when we stand firm against vice and
immorality and stand humbly but assuredly with God and the
"cloud of witnesses" (Hebrews 12:1) made up of Saints on both
sides of the veil (2 Kings 6:16; compare 1 John 4:4).

During World War II many Latter-day Saints in European
countries wondered if the time had come for them to leave their
homelands and "gather to Zion," that is, to relocate to Salt Lake
City or somewhere else in the United States. Elder Harold B. Lee
addressed himself to such persons when he said: "I know now
that the place of safety in this world is not in any given place;
it doesn't make so much difference *where* we live; but the all-
important thing is *how we live*, and I have found that security
can come to Israel only when they keep the commandments,
when they live so that they can enjoy the companionship, the
direction, the comfort, and the guidance of the Holy Spirit of the

Lord, when they are willing to listen to these men whom God has set here to preside as His mouthpieces, and when we obey the counsels of the Church."[5]

Professor Rasmussen observed: "To most questions man wants to have an answer. But to the Lord's question man must *be* an answer. From man God does not need information. Man's response must be man's own self. As each human being is different, so will be each response."[6]

"Adam, where art thou? Eve, where goest thou?" (Genesis 3:9). We answer those questions as we face the right way, as we demonstrate our loyalty and allegiance to the kingdom of God by giving him our heart as well as our word. By so doing, we stand in holy places, and we will not be moved.

Chapter 10

LOOKING FORTH FOR
THE GREAT DAY

*H*ow should we as members of the Church of Jesus Christ feel about the fact that we do indeed live in the eleventh hour, the Saturday night of time? How does it make us feel to know that we are living through an era when more and more of the prophecies are being fulfilled? The Savior declared to Sidney Rigdon: "The poor and the meek shall have the gospel preached unto them, and they shall be looking forth for the time of my coming, for it is nigh at hand—and they shall learn the parable of the fig tree, for even now already summer is nigh" (D&C 35:15–16). Three months later the Prophet received the revelation recorded as section 45 of the Doctrine and Covenants, an oracle that makes known many of the signs of the times. "Ye look and behold the fig trees," the Lord said, "and ye see them with your eyes, and ye say when they begin to shoot forth, and their leaves are yet tender, that summer is now nigh at hand; even so it shall be in that day when they shall see all these things, then shall they know that the hour is nigh. And it shall come to pass that he that feareth me shall be looking forth for the great day of the Lord to come, even for the signs of the coming of the Son of Man" (D&C

51

45:37–39). In other words, the faithful will look forward to the Lord's advent with excitement and sweet anticipation.

One of the challenges we face is to anticipate that day without obsessing over it. We should study and reflect deeply on the holy word concerning what lies ahead, not so that we can chronicle and correlate and prepare formulas and distribute lists and set forth specific schedules but rather so that we can prepare our souls properly for that sublime occasion. We might well ask ourselves, "Our Lord and Savior is coming. What do I need to do *today* to prepare myself for *tomorrow?* What efforts can I make now to ensure that when he does come he will see my face with pleasure? What kinds of activities might I be engaged in that will cause me to feel comfortable and confident at that time? What elements in my life and lifestyle, person and personality, need to be jettisoned for me to enjoy that measure of spiritual enlightenment so desperately needed in these last days?" Interestingly, the three parables of preparation found in Matthew 25 point toward specific things you and I can do to better prepare ourselves, our families, and those under our charge to welcome the coming Lord.

Jesus taught: "Blessed are those servants, whom the Lord when he cometh shall find watching; for he shall gird himself, and make them to sit down to meat, and will come forth and serve them. For, behold, he cometh in the first watch of the night, and he shall also come in the second watch, and again he shall come in the third watch. And verily I say unto you, *He hath already come,* as it is written of him" (JST, Luke 12:40–42; emphasis added). What a strange statement! How is it that our Lord comes in the first watch of the night and also in the second and third watches? In addition, how has he come already?

Elder Bruce R. McConkie offered the following insights: "One of the great incentives which encourages and entices men to live lives of personal righteousness, is the doctrine of the Second Coming of the Messiah. Many revelations speak of the signs which shall precede our Lord's return; others tell of the tragic yet glorious events which shall attend and accompany his return to earth; and still others recite the good and ill which shall befall the living and the dead at that time. All this is preserved in holy writ so that men will be led to prepare themselves for the day of the Lord, the day when he shall take vengeance upon the ungodly and pour forth blessings upon those who love his appearing. (D&C 133:50–52; 2 Thessalonians 1:7–10) . . .

"All of the Lord's ministers, all of the members of his Church, and for that matter all men everywhere ('What I say unto one, I say unto all'), are counseled to await with righteousness the coming of the Lord. However, most men will die before he comes, and only those then living will rejoice or tremble, as the case may be, at his personal presence. But all who did prepare will be rewarded as though they had lived when he came, while the wicked will be 'cut asunder' and appointed their 'portion with the hypocrites' as surely as though they lived in the very day of dread and vengeance.

"Thus, in effect, the Lord comes in every watch of the night, on every occasion when men are called to face death and judgment."[1]

Keeping an eye on the *end* almost always helps one to deal properly with the *means*. Or, stated differently, being aware of what lies ahead can be extremely valuable in knowing how best to handle challenging circumstances and trying situations now. If my marriage is performed by one holding the sealing power, when the sealer marries my wife and me "for time and all eternity," I am much more likely to focus my attention on building a strong and enduring relationship than if the ceremony were merely a civil ordinance "till death do you part." Knowing that families are intended to span the veil of death and continue everlastingly motivates me to make an appreciable effort to forgive, assume the best, and labor unceasingly to make our home a bit of heaven on earth and the members of the household a forever family. Stephen R. Covey taught simply, "Begin with the end in mind."[2]

In speaking of the Lord's coming in glory and considering what events must transpire, the apostle Peter asked, "What manner of persons ought ye to be in all holy conversation and godliness, *looking for and hasting unto the coming of the day of God,* wherein the heavens being on fire shall be dissolved, and the elements shall melt with fervent heat?" (2 Peter 3:11–12; emphasis added). The New International Version renders the same passage as follows: "Since everything will be destroyed in this way, what kind of people ought you to be? You ought to live holy and godly lives *as you look forward to the day of God and speed its coming.*" While the day of Christ's second coming is no doubt as set as was the day of the his first coming,[3] there are things we can do to hasten our own righteous preparation and hurry along the establishment of Zion.

In January 1831 the Lord Jesus addressed himself to James Covill, a Methodist minister who demonstrated briefly an interest in the restored gospel. "Go forth baptizing with water, preparing the way before my face for the time of my coming; for the time is at hand; the day or the hour no man knoweth; but it surely shall come. And he that receiveth these things receiveth me; and they shall be gathered unto me in time and in eternity. And again, it shall come to pass that on as many as ye shall baptize with water, ye shall lay your hands, and *they shall receive the gift of the Holy Ghost, and shall be looking forth for the signs of my coming, and shall know me*" (D&C 39:20–23; emphasis added). Truly, those members of the Church of Jesus Christ who cultivate the gift of the Holy Ghost and enjoy its sweet fruits—these are they who will have come to be like him and who will then, in that great day, see Christ as he is (1 John 3:1–2). And they will know him.

Chapter 11
ZION'S BEAUTIFUL GARMENTS

I have noted with sadness an increasing informality of dress in sacred settings. When I have visited other Christian churches, I have observed how common it is for congregants to wear Levi's, shorts, T-shirts, tank tops, and flip-flops. And, unfortunately, it is not uncommon to see similar trends among Latter-day Saints. Casualness in dress too often reflects a casualness toward spiritual things. It may not be true for others, but I personally have found that how I dress affects how I feel and how I act. There's a reason why, for generations, men and women and boys and girls dressed in their Sunday best for church. It was a sign of reverence, of respect for holy things, an outward manifestation that inwardly we were prepared to be taught the gospel, to be inspired, to enter into the realm of divine experience. It is for this reason that our Church leaders have encouraged priesthood holders who are officiating in the ordinances to wear a white shirt and tie. While we do not want to obsess over shirt colors, fixate over outward measures of faithfulness, or scold or embarrass those who may not so dress (whether by choice or because they cannot afford to), there is wisdom in looking the part.

Jacob, son of Lehi, spoke of the state of persons at the time of resurrection, when "the spirit and the body is restored to itself again, and all men become incorruptible, and immortal." He declared, "Wherefore, we shall have a perfect knowledge of all our guilt, and our uncleanness, and our nakedness; and the righteous shall have a perfect knowledge of their enjoyment, and their righteousness, *being clothed with purity, yea, even with the robe of righteousness*" (2 Nephi 9:13–14; emphasis added). This is a marvelous expression: to be "clothed with purity" and to be adorned in the "robe of righteousness" are surely what Latter-day Saints desire for their family forever. We aspire to purity. We covet righteousness, for we know that these attributes and qualities bring peace and joy in this world and eternal life in the world to come (D&C 59:23).

In warning the Saints in the branch of the Church at Sardis, the Lord Jesus Christ spoke of the need to be spiritually vigilant: "Be watchful, . . . for I have not found thy works perfect before God." The Master then called upon the early disciples to "hold fast, and repent. If therefore thou shalt not watch, I will come on thee as a thief, and thou shalt not know what hour I will come upon thee. Thou hast a few names even in Sardis which have not defiled their garments; and *they shall walk with me in white: for they are worthy.* He that overcometh, the same shall be *clothed in white raiment*; and I will not blot out his name out of the book of life, but I will confess his name before my Father, and before his angels" (Revelation 3:2–5; emphasis added).

Later, in reporting on the fate of the Christian martyrs, John the Revelator wrote: "And when he had opened the fifth seal [the period of time from the mortal ministry of Christ to A.D. 1000], I saw under the altar the souls of them that were slain for the word of God, and for the testimony which they held. . . . And white robes were given unto every one of them" (Revelation 6:9–11).

John later records that when Christ the Bridegroom returns, the bride, meaning the Church, will be "arrayed in fine linen, clean and white; for the fine linen is the righteousness of saints" (Revelation 19:8).

With these thoughts in mind, let us now turn to a related passage, this time from the Old Testament. Jehovah calls out to his chosen people: "Awake, awake; put on thy strength, O Zion; put on thy beautiful garments, O Jerusalem, the holy city: for henceforth there shall no more come into thee the uncircumcised and the unclean. Shake thyself from the dust; arise, and sit down, O Jerusalem: loose thyself from the bands of thy neck, O captive daughter of Zion. For thus saith the Lord, Ye have sold yourselves for nought; and ye shall be redeemed without money" (Isaiah 52:1–3). This is a sobering call to repentance, an invitation to be reconciled (to sit down with again), an encouragement to be gathered, an inducement to come unto Jehovah, receive his gospel, apply his atonement, partake of that salvation which is free, that everlasting life which comes only through the merits and mercy and grace of the Holy Messiah (2 Nephi 2:4, 8; 9:50–51; 31:19). It is also a poignant prophecy of what Jehovah will do in the last days to ransom Israel.

On one occasion, Joseph Smith and some of his associates participated in an inspired question-and-answer session. "Questions by Elias Higbee: What is meant by the command in Isaiah, 52d chapter, 1st verse, which saith: Put on thy strength, O Zion—and what people had Isaiah reference to?" Note the revealed answer: "He had reference to *those whom God should call in the last days, who should hold the power of priesthood* to bring again Zion, and the redemption of Israel; and *to put on her strength is to put on the authority of the priesthood*, which she, Zion, has a right to by lineage [see D&C 86:8–10]; *and to return to that power which she had lost*" (D&C 113:7–8; emphasis added).

How much more powerfully could the Lord our God appeal to us, as citizens of Zion, to spread the message of the Restoration and thereby to contribute to the gathering of Israel? How could the God of Israel plead with more power to those *authorized* to act in his name to go out of Babylon, to rise above the foolishness of the world, to cast off the barnacles of sin, and to put on that *power* of the priesthood that comes only through faithful observance of the commandments?

Elias Higbee followed up with another question: "What are we to understand by Zion loosing herself from the bands of her neck; 2d verse?" Then comes the reply: "We are to understand that the scattered remnants are exhorted to *return to the Lord from whence they have fallen; which if they do, the promise of the Lord is that he will speak to them, or give them revelation.* . . . The bands of her neck are the curses of God upon her, or the remnants of Israel in their scattered condition among the Gentiles" (D&C 113:9–10; emphasis added). The people of Israel, individually as well as the entire nation collectively, are scattered whenever they reject the Lord and his gospel, when they settle for second best, when they compromise and concede, when they sell their birthright for a mess of pottage. They are then scattered in the sense that, spiritually speaking, they have cut themselves off from the Spirit of God and do not enjoy the close association, the sweet fellowship, and the loving loyalty that ought to exist between a covenant God and his covenant people. They become, in the words of the apostle Paul, "aliens from the commonwealth of Israel, and strangers from the covenants of promise, having no hope, and without God in the world" (Ephesians 2:12).

But the Christ of the Covenant provides a highway of

righteousness (Isaiah 11:16; 35:8) by which the wanderers may return: through exercising faith in him who is the Mediator of the new covenant, repenting sorely of sins and sinfulness, being baptized and confirmed and demonstrating covenant loyalty thereafter, and, finally, dedicating themselves to the ministry of being a light to the world (Isaiah 49:6; Matthew 5:14). "But now in Christ Jesus ye who sometimes were far off are made nigh by the blood of Christ. . . . Now therefore ye are no more strangers and foreigners, but fellowcitizens with the saints, and of the household of God; and are built upon the foundation of the apostles and prophets, Jesus Christ himself being the chief corner stone" (Ephesians 2:13, 19–20).

The Book of Mormon bears an incomparable witness that through faith in our Lord we may have our garments made white in the blood of the Lamb (1 Nephi 12:10). Alma explained that "there can no man be saved except his garments are washed white; yea, his garments must be purified until they are cleansed from all stain, through the blood of him of whom it has been spoken by our fathers, who should come to redeem his people from their sins" (Alma 5:21). Alma implored his people to come back into the covenant family: "And may the Lord bless you, and *keep your garments spotless, that ye may at last be brought to sit down* [reconciled] *with Abraham, Isaac, and Jacob,* and the holy prophets who have been ever since the world began, *having your garments spotless even as their garments are spotless,* in the kingdom of heaven to go no more out" (Alma 7:25; emphasis added; see also 3 Nephi 27:19; Ether 13:11).

As a part of the remarkable dedicatory prayer of the Kirtland Temple, Joseph Smith pleaded with God that the members of the Church might "be adorned as a bride for that day when thou shalt unveil the heavens, and cause the mountains to flow down at thy presence, . . . that our garments may be pure, that we may be clothed upon with robes of righteousness, with palms in our hands, and crowns of glory upon our heads, and reap eternal joy for all our sufferings" (D&C 109:74–76). As we who have received the principles and ordinances of the gospel extend ourselves in service and rid ourselves of the profane, the unnecessary, and the spiritually distracting, we begin to gain spiritual *power*, power to lighten the heavy burdens of our brothers and sisters; power to enjoy and use the gifts of the Spirit; power to bless the lives of our friends and loved ones; power to lift conversations from the mundane to the meaningful; power to speak the word of the Lord and cause it to go down into the hearts of those who listen, where it will burn like fire; power to provide for our families and those over whom we may have charge a vision of eternal life and the sweet assurance that we can make it. "For Zion must increase in beauty, and in holiness; her borders must be enlarged; her stakes must be strengthened; yea, verily I say unto you, Zion must arise and put on her beautiful garments" (D&C 82:14). It is time to clothe ourselves in righteousness.

Chapter 12
CONFIDENT WHEN HE COMES

In one of my classes recently, a study of Acts through Revelation in the New Testament, we talked for a while during our discussion of 1 Thessalonians 4 about the second coming of Jesus Christ and how best to prepare for that day. A number of students expressed some nervousness about that day, which will be either great or terrible, and one student indicated, with a smile on his face, that he would prefer that it be postponed indefinitely.

"Tell us more," I said. "Why put it off? Why wish that it would never come? Is it just because our lives are out of order, that we have some serious repenting to do?"

We agreed that if we were hiding deep sin, the coming of the Lord would be the last thing we would want to have happen. One of the young women spoke. "While my life isn't exactly where it needs to be," she said, "I don't think I am totally unworthy. I hold a temple recommend and use it regularly, but I'm still somewhat frightened by the thought that the Savior might come tonight or tomorrow or a week from now."

I didn't let the matter rest. "Why is that?" I inquired. The comments that began to come from the students were revealing. These were outstanding young Latter-day Saints, but they felt some discomfort about the Second Coming, for at least the following reasons: (1) they hadn't had the opportunity to marry, raise a family, and live to an old age; (2) some of their family members had strayed from the path of right, and they wanted more time to try to recover them; and (3) they were just a bit unsure about their own standing before God.

I tried to respond to their first two fears by reassuring them that there is plenty of time for them to live a long and productive family life and that they should seek to buy a home, purchase insurance, plant cherry trees, and continue to pray and labor in behalf of those who have wandered. Such prayers would not go unnoticed or unattended to by a merciful and all-loving Lord (James 5:16). I reiterated the teachings of current Church leaders that while the coming of the Lord is indeed something we each need to prepare for, it is not something we need to either fear or dread.

Attending to the third concern required a bit more time, but it proved to be worth the effort. In general, we spoke of what the influence and power of the Holy Ghost in our lives signified: that we are on course, in covenant, that the Lord is pleased with the course we are pursuing, and that if we continue to move in that same direction, eternal life will eventually be ours. I stressed that it was important to hold a current temple recommend, that worthiness to participate in the covenants and ordinances of the house of the Lord—the earthly counterpart to paradise, the abode of the righteous hereafter—is worthiness to inherit the celestial kingdom in the world to come.

The Prophet Joseph Smith taught in the School of the Elders that three conditions must exist before one can exercise faith unto life and salvation: (1) "the idea that [God] actually exists"; (2) "a *correct* idea of his character, perfections, and attributes";

and (3) a "knowledge that the course of life which [one] is pursuing is according" to the will of God.[1] The first two prerequisites for saving faith clearly have something to do with *how well we understand God*. But the third has much to do with *what we understand about ourselves*. The first two entail a fixed and settled confidence in the Lord our God, in his knowledge and qualities and powers. But the third is largely about our confidence in how well *we* are complying with the will of God.

President David O. McKay taught that "spirituality is the consciousness of victory over self, and of communion with the Infinite."[2] It isn't just that we have been victorious over self but also that we are *conscious* or *aware* of that victory. Of course our trust and confidence must always be in Jesus Christ; we must rely wholly, rely alone upon the merits of him who is mighty to save (2 Nephi 31:19; Moroni 6:4). This is what we call faith in the Lord Jesus Christ. But there is an element of faith associated with a kind of confidence in how well we have complied with God's will, not a confidence that produces haughtiness or arrogance but rather a quiet assurance that God is pleased with us. As President Hugh B. Brown pointed out, God didn't need to learn anything about Abraham when the latter was commanded to offer his covenant son, Isaac, in sacrifice; "*Abraham* needed to learn something about Abraham."[3] Abraham needed to know, from personal and painful experience, that there was not anything the Lord would ask of him that he would not be willing to do.

The apostle Paul wrote to encourage the early Saints: "Take heed, brethren, lest there be in any of you an evil heart of unbelief, in departing from the living God. But *exhort one another daily, while it is called To day*; lest any of you be hardened through the deceitfulness of sin. For *we are made partakers of Christ, if we hold the beginning of our confidence stedfast unto the end*; while it

is said, To day if ye will hear his voice, harden not your hearts"
(Hebrews 3:12–15; emphasis added). In what has become one of
my favorite biblical passages, taken from that same epistle, Paul
wrote: "It is a fearful thing to fall into the hands of the living
God. But call to remembrance the former days, in which, after
ye were illuminated [after the Spirit had witnessed to you of the
truthfulness of the gospel], ye endured a great fight of afflictions.
. . . For ye had compassion of me in my bonds, and took joyfully
the spoiling of your goods, *knowing in yourselves that ye have in
heaven a better and an enduring substance. Cast not away therefore
your confidence,* which hath great recompence of reward. For ye
have need of patience, that, after ye have done the will of God,
ye might receive the promise. For yet a little while, and he that
shall come will come, and will not tarry" (Hebrews 10:31–37;
emphasis added).

That is another way of saying you have received the divine
witness: You know of the truthfulness of the gospel, you know
that Christ will come again, and so don't lose the confidence you
have had since the beginning. This is obviously a confidence in
the Lord himself, but also implied is the quiet but real sense that
you really are celestial material. Elder Jeffrey R. Holland beck-
oned to the Latter-day Saints: "I wish to encourage every one
of us regarding the opposition that so often comes after enlight-
ened decisions have been made, after moments of revelation and
conviction have given us peace and an assurance we thought we
would never lose.

" . . . Don't panic and retreat. Don't lose your confidence.
Don't forget how you once felt. Don't distrust the experience you
had. That tenacity is what saved Moses and Joseph Smith when
the adversary confronted them, and it is what will save you.

" . . . With any major decision there are cautions and

considerations to make, but once there has been illumination, beware the temptation to retreat from a good thing. If it was right when you prayed about it and trusted it and lived for it, it is right now. Don't give up when the pressure mounts."[4]

The Prophet Joseph Smith's counsel from Liberty Jail regarding how members of the Lord's Church should lead and direct others is poignant and profound. We are taught that it is by persuasion, long-suffering, gentleness, meekness, love unfeigned, kindness, pure knowledge, and inspired reproof that righteous leadership can be effective. In addition, the Prophet wrote, "Let thy bowels also be full of *charity* towards all men, and to the household of faith, and let *virtue* garnish thy thoughts unceasingly; *then shall thy confidence wax strong in the presence of God; and the doctrine of the priesthood shall distil upon thy soul as the dews from heaven*" (D&C 121:45; emphasis added; see vv. 41–44).

As we look ahead to the Second Advent, we find John's counsel extremely pertinent: "And now, little children, abide in him; that, *when he shall appear, we may have confidence*, and not be ashamed before him at his coming" (1 John 2:28; emphasis added). Let us face the future with sweet assurance, "being confident of this very thing, that he which hath begun a good work in you will perform [complete, accomplish] it until the day of Jesus Christ" (Philippians 1:6). Indeed, God is working within us, working on our wills and our behaviors. Let us, therefore, join with our Maker in saving our soul and working out our salvation "with fear and trembling" (Philippians 2:12–13).

Chapter 13

THE GOSPEL PREACHED
IN ALL THE WORLD

*B*efore his final ascension into heaven, the risen Lord said to his disciples: "Go ye therefore, and teach [make disciples of] all nations, baptizing them in the name of the Father, and of the Son, and of the Holy Ghost: teaching them to observe all things whatsoever I have commanded you: and, lo, I am with you alway, even unto the end of the world" (Matthew 28:19–20). Mark records this instruction a bit differently: "Go ye into all the world, and preach the gospel to every creature. He that believeth and is baptized shall be saved; but he that believeth not shall be damned" (Mark 16:15–16). This is what the Christian world has come to know as the Great Commission, and it is the reason the followers of Christ evangelize, proselytize, and seek to bring into people's lives the blessings of the gospel of Jesus Christ.

That same commission came to the members of the restored Church in these words: "Go ye into all the world, preach the gospel to every creature, *acting in the authority which I have given you*, baptizing in the name of the Father, and of the Son, and of the Holy Ghost. And he that believeth and is baptized shall be saved, and he that believeth not shall be damned" (D&C 68:8–9; emphasis added). Further, we of the latter days have been told that "the sound must go forth from this place into all the world, and unto the uttermost parts of the earth—the gospel must be preached unto every creature, with signs following them that believe" (D&C 58:64). And so it is that the Latter-day Saints, from the days of young Samuel Harrison Smith, brother of the Prophet Joseph, have had the proclamation of the gospel as a principal duty.

We have proclaimed the gospel in the face of opposition from some who are angered that we should choose to send missionaries to the "saved," to those who are already Christian. Our response to that criticism is quite simple: We do not always know who has been "saved," who has already received the message of Christ and sought to incorporate his atonement in their lives. Consequently, we go to everyone, to every nation that will allow us to enter. But of course that is only a partial answer. We believe that with the deaths of the original apostles, divine priesthood authority—apostolic authority—was lost from the earth, and many plain and precious truths were taken away or kept back from the Bible, causing many in the world to stumble (1 Nephi 13:24–29). We as members of the restored Church believe we have something precious, something of inestimable worth, to offer to the world— namely, the knowledge that priesthood authority and doctrinal truths have been restored to earth through the ministry of heavenly messengers and the call of modern apostles and prophets. Given how significant this message is, how pertinent it is to the world's need to identify and cherish truth, how could we not want to bear our witness of the Restoration?

We appreciate that one of the signs of the times is spoken of as follows: "And again, this Gospel of the Kingdom shall be preached in all the world, for a witness unto all nations, and then shall the end come, or the destruction of the wicked" (Joseph Smith– Matthew 1:31). "All the world" in Jesus' day would certainly have included the Roman Empire and even reached beyond its confines; Christian legends speak of various apostles carrying the gospel message to Africa, to India, to China, etc. In our own day, I have watched with wonder over the past half century as barriers have been removed, walls and curtains have come down, and impediments to the spread of Christianity have been divinely dissolved.

As a teenager, I never imagined that I would see such a thing. Hearing the premier of the Soviet Union warn the American people in the 1960s that "we will bury you" convinced me that Russians and many eastern Europeans and East Germans and millions of Chinese would need to wait until the millennial day to be taught the gospel. But only thirty years later, one of my dearest friends, Richard Chapple, was called to preside over the mission in Moscow, Russia, with his wife, Suzanne, as his companion. Two more of my favorite people, Bill and Cathy Clark, served two humanitarian missions to Mongolia. One of my colleagues in Religious Education, Daniel Judd, served as president of the mission in Accra, Ghana, in West Africa, with his wife, Kay, as his companion. How marvelous are the ways of the Lord! And this is but the beginning of what shall yet be.

At the sesquicentennial anniversary of the organization of The Church of Jesus Christ of Latter-day Saints in the April 1980 general conference, Elder Bruce R. McConkie prophesied: "Looking ahead, we see the gospel preached in all nations and to every people with success attending.

"We see the Lord break down the barriers so that the world of Islam and the world of Communism can hear the message of the restoration; and we glory in the fact that Ishmael—as well as Isaac—and Esau—as well as Jacob—shall have an inheritance in the eternal kingdom.

"We see congregations of the covenant people worshipping

the Lord in Moscow and Peking and Saigon. We see Saints of the Most High raising their voices in Egypt and India and Africa.

"We see stakes of Zion in all parts of the earth; and Israel, the chosen people, gathering into these cities of holiness, as it were, to await the coming of their King. . . .

"We see the Saints of God, who are scattered upon all the face of the earth, rise in power and glory and stand as lights and guides to the people of their own nations.

"We see our children and our children's children stand firm in defense of truth and virtue, crowned with the power of God, carrying off the kingdom triumphantly.

"We see the faithful Saints perfecting their lives and preparing for the coming of him whose children they are, preparing for the glorious mansion he has promised them in the kingdom of his Father."[1]

For far too long, it has been our practice to encourage member missionary work in the wards and branches with invitations like this: "Come on, brothers and sisters, let's do our part; we need to help these missionaries do their job of bringing people into the Church." Yet that is exactly backwards: it is *our* job to do missionary work; the full-time missionaries are called, set apart, and sent to our congregations to *help us* do our job. As local members and residents of an area, we are the finders, and they, the missionaries, are the teachers.

It is our charge to pray earnestly to receive the spirit of our calling as member missionaries. Our plea to the Almighty is that he will open our minds and our hearts and endow us with a portion of his divine love toward those not of our faith, banish fear and hesitation from our hearts, and assist us to feel more natural and more settled, secure, and confident in initiating gospel conversations. This Church will not witness the kind of harvest of souls foreseen by ancient and modern prophets as long as we continue to assume that the burden for missionary work rests upon the shoulders of a relatively small number of full-time missionaries. The greater responsibility rests with us. "And again, I say unto you, I give unto you a commandment, that every man, both elder, priest, teacher, and also member, go to with his might, with the labor of his hands, to prepare and accomplish the things which I have commanded. And let your preaching be the warning voice, every man to his neighbor, in mildness and in meekness" (D&C 38:40–41).

As a significant part of the Abrahamic covenant, the father of the faithful was promised that his descendants would be the means by which the gospel of salvation would be taken to the peoples of the earth (Abraham 2:8–11). More specifically, the tribes of Ephraim and Manasseh were charged anciently to "push the people together to the ends of the earth" (Deuteronomy 33:17), and that same charge has been renewed in the dispensation of the fulness of times (D&C 58:45).

And to show that even many of Ephraim are yet to be gathered, a revelation affirms: "Then cometh the day when the arm of the Lord shall be revealed in power in convincing *the nations, the heathen nations, the house of Joseph,* of the gospel of their salvation. For it shall come to pass in that day"—our day and the days to come—"that every man shall hear the fulness of the gospel in his own tongue, and in his own language, through those who are ordained unto this power" (D&C 90:10–11; emphasis added; compare 133:8–9).

Those who have enjoyed the inspiring and sanctifying power of the gospel of Jesus Christ in their lives, who have undergone the mighty change that accompanies membership in the Church of Jesus Christ and the receipt of the gift of the Holy Ghost, cannot help but want others to enjoy the same sweet privileges. Like the sons of Mosiah, "they [are] desirous that salvation should be declared to every creature, for they [cannot] bear that any human soul should perish; yea, even the very thoughts that any soul should endure endless torment [causes] them to quake and tremble" (Mosiah 28:3). And so because we love our friends and neighbors, as well as the billions we do not know, we seek to share what we have with them. And this will continue until the day comes when there are a hundred million Latter-day Saints,[2] indeed, until Jesus returns in glory. And it will continue with even greater intensity during the Millennium (3 Nephi 21:25–29).

In describing some of the trying and even frightful times incident to the Master's appearance, Elder Bruce R. McConkie wrote: "The signs in heaven above are like nothing man has ever seen. Blood is everywhere; fire and vapors of smoke fill the atmospheric heavens. No man has seen a rainbow this year.

" . . . And above all are the vexing words of those Mormon Elders! They are everywhere preaching their strange doctrine, saying that the coming of the Lord is near, and that unless men repent and believe the gospel they will be destroyed by the brightness of his coming.

"In this setting, as these and ten thousand like things are in progress, suddenly, quickly, as from the midst of eternity, He comes!"[3]

The Savior will bring in his millennial reign and with it a new era of missionary work. In a very real sense, the work of the gathering of Israel then *commences* (3 Nephi 21:25–29)—that is, all previous gatherings will seem to pale in significance. Truly, as Joseph the Seer pointed out, "After all that has been said, the greatest and most important duty is to preach the Gospel."[4] We pray for guidance and courage, and then we reach out—we have a world to help save.

Chapter 14
"ISRAEL SHALL BE SAVED"

During the first decade of my teaching at Brigham Young University, it was my privilege to teach the Book of Mormon many times. Those years proved to be formative ones, as they became foundational to my understanding of the restored gospel and aided immeasurably in my grasp of the great teachings of the Holy Bible. During the second semester of a rather large section of Book of Mormon, a young woman in class asked, "Brother Millet, there's a phrase that is found throughout the Book of Mormon that I really don't understand"

I responded, "What phrase is that?"

She replied, "The house of Israel."

Let me put this question into perspective. We were then in 3 Nephi in our study. This young woman was one of the brightest students in the class and had done exceptionally well both semesters. I learned later that she came from an outstanding Latter-day Saint family and had taken early-morning seminary for four years. Her question was sobering. It caused me to wonder how many of the other ninety students might have had similar questions but were hesitant to raise them.

This particular semester was especially memorable because

of a similar incident in another of my Book of Mormon classes, this one designated for returned missionaries. One of the young men asked, "Brother Millet, what difference does it make that my patriarchal blessing states that I am a descendant of Ephraim?"

"Anyone else have this question?" I asked.

Several others in the class nodded.

Once again I was staggered by the question. I wondered how such outstanding young Latter-day Saints could have come that far, some even having served full-time missions, without understanding the identity, responsibility, and destiny of the house of Israel.

I have reflected many times on the opening line of the tenth article of faith: "We believe in the literal gathering of Israel." Why would the Prophet have stated it this way? For one thing, by the time of Joseph Smith—and this is even more true today—most in the religious world, particularly Christians, had come to speak of Israel as meaning the Jews only or as being merely a symbolic description of those who had come into the Christian church. The doctrine in the promise made to Abraham that his seed would be a leavening influence throughout the world (Genesis 13; 15; 17) was all but lost. Indeed, one of the vital things lost during periods of apostasy is individuals' sense of covenant consciousness—who they are and Whose they are. Through Joseph Smith, God determined not only to restore the holy priesthood and many plain and precious doctrinal truths but also to bring his children "to the knowledge of their fathers . . . and also to the knowledge of my covenants, saith the Lord" (2 Nephi 3:12).

The scriptures teach that in our first estate, our premortal existence, some exercised exceedingly great faith and performed many good works (Alma 13:3). In the words of Elder Melvin J. Ballard, Israel is "a group of souls tested, tried, and proven before they were born into the world. . . . Through this lineage were to come the true and tried souls that had demonstrated their righteousness in the spirit world before they came here."[1] These sacred truths were taught by Moses (Deuteronomy 32:7–9) and the apostle Paul (Acts 17:24, 26). It thus appears that the declaration of lineage by patriarchs is as much a statement about who and what we were as it is about who we are now and what we may become.

Through the generations of Israelite history, the descendants of Abraham, Isaac, and Jacob moved in and out of favor with God; that is, they vacillated between being a scattered people and a gathered people. When they forsook the worship of Jehovah and his doctrine, they were scattered in that they lost the Spirit of God and were alienated from the people of the covenant and, in some cases, were displaced from the lands of their inheritance into strange lands, often the lands of the captors (1 Nephi 22:3–5; 2 Nephi 6:8–11; 10:1–6). When they humbled themselves and turned their hearts once again to the Holy One of Israel, they were gathered again, first spiritually and then temporally. They were gathered first and foremost to God, to Christ, to the gospel, to the true Church. In addition, they were allowed to reclaim the lands of their inheritance (Isaiah 43:1–6; Jeremiah 16:14–18; 31:31–34; 2 Nephi 6:11; 9:1–2; 10:7–8).

In our day, God's covenant people, the people of Israel, are gathered one by one when they receive the message of the restored gospel, repent of their sins, accept baptism and confirmation at the hands of those holding proper authority, and continue faithful to their covenants. We gather Israel through missionary work. The work of gathering Israel will accelerate in the last days. "And now I show unto you a parable," Jesus said. "Behold, wheresoever the carcass is, there will the eagles be gathered together;

so likewise shall mine elect be gathered from the four quarters of the earth" (Joseph Smith–Matthew 1:27). Very early in this dispensation the elders were instructed, "And ye are called to bring to pass the gathering of mine elect; for mine elect hear my voice and harden not their hearts" (D&C 29:7).

In a revelation given to Joseph Smith and Sidney Rigdon, the Lord declared, "Keep all the commandments and covenants by which ye are bound; and I will cause the heavens to shake for your good, and Satan shall tremble and Zion shall rejoice upon the hills and flourish; and *Israel shall be saved in mine own due time;* and by the keys which I have given shall they be led, and no more be confounded at all" (D&C 35:24–25; emphasis added). The Lord affirmed a short time later that "I have a great work laid up in store, for *Israel shall be saved,* and I will lead them whithersoever I will, and no power shall stay my hand" (D&C 38:33; emphasis added).

In the early days of the Church, when persons chose to be baptized, they began planning to gather, to relocate, to where the body of the Latter-day Saints resided. They moved themselves to Missouri, to Illinois, and to the Great Basin. This was absolutely necessary in the early days of the Restoration so that a nucleus of faithful members might become a center of strength against persecution and against evil, a center for missionary work from which the proclamation of truth could go forth (D&C 58:64). Tens of thousands of British Saints, for example, gathered to the western United States as soon as they could afford the journey. These beloved people became a godsend, a base upon which the restored Church could build. This physical gathering continued until the end of the nineteenth century, when the First Presidency of the Church began to call upon the members, far and wide, to remain in their homelands, to establish and strengthen their stakes, and thereby to build Zion throughout the world. Beginning at that time, persons who joined the Church complied with the law of gathering by being baptized into the Church and then congregating with the faithful in their immediate vicinity.

In what has become a kind of doctrinal benchmark, Elder Bruce R. McConkie addressed the Saints in an area conference in Mexico and Central America in August 1972: "This gathering has commenced and shall continue until the righteous are assembled into the congregations of the Saints in all nations of the earth." And then, becoming more specific, Elder McConkie pointed out that "the place of gathering for the Mexican Saints is in Mexico; the place of gathering for the Guatemalan Saints is in Guatemala; the place of gathering for the Brazilian Saints is in Brazil; and so it goes throughout the length and breadth of the whole earth. Japan is for the Japanese; Korea is for the Koreans; Australia is for the Australians; every nation is the gathering place for its own people."[2] President Harold B. Lee quoted that address in his own remarks during the October 1973 general conference, stating his agreement with Elder McConkie.[3] Years later, President Boyd K. Packer noted that President Lee's statement had, "in effect, announced that the pioneering phase of gathering was now over. The gathering is now to be out of the world into the Church in every nation."[4]

There is an aspect of the gathering of Israel that is particularly appealing and comforting to my wife, Shauna, and me. As much as parents try to hold their children close; as diligent as they may be in praying, reading scripture, and attending church; as much as they may support their children in music, dance concerts, or athletic events; and as deeply as they long to rear to maturity solid, active, involved, and committed Latter-day Saints, some children along the way lose track of who they are and wander from the path of faithfulness. In a church in which family is everything, in which the continuation of the family unit into eternity is a vital dimension of eternal life, nothing could be more painful, more spiritually stressful, than helplessly watching a loved one choose unwisely and foreclose future opportunities.

But the prophets have not left us without hope. The risen Lord, in speaking to his American Hebrews, affirmed: "Ye are the children of the prophets; and *ye are of the house of Israel; and ye are of the covenant which the Father made with your fathers,* saying unto Abraham: And in thy seed shall all the kindreds of the earth be blessed. The Father having raised me up unto you first, and *sent me to bless you in turning away every one of you from his iniquities; and this because ye are the children of the covenant*" (3 Nephi 20:25–26; emphasis added).

I was inspired and consoled by the teachings of Elder Jeffrey R. Holland as he applied a scriptural passage in a way different from anything I had ever before heard or even imagined. In offering comfort and consolation to parents whose children have wandered, Elder Holland read from Doctrine and Covenants 101 and asked his listeners to view those teachings in light of their own families and homes. The Lord declares in verse 11: "Mine indignation is soon to be poured out without measure upon all nations; and this will I do when the cup of their iniquity is full." Elder Holland taught: "'And in that day, all who are found upon the watch-tower, or in other words, *all mine Israel,'*—that's you and your children—'*shall be saved* [compare Paul's words in Romans 11:26]. *And they that have been scattered shall be gathered'*—even a child that strays will be reclaimed. '*And all they who have mourned'*—including parents about family circumstances—'*shall be comforted.'*"[5] The scripture continues: "Therefore, let your hearts be comforted concerning Zion [think of individual homes]; for all flesh is in mine hands; be still and know that I am God. Zion shall not be moved out of her place, notwithstanding her children are scattered. They that remain, and are pure in heart, *shall return, and come to their inheritances, they and their children, with songs of everlasting joy,* to build up the waste places of Zion—and all these things that the prophets might be fulfilled" (D&C 101:11–19; emphasis added).

We are of Israel. We are a covenant people, men and women under covenant. Those of us who bear the holy priesthood have received the covenant of the Melchizedek Priesthood and have surely read and reflected on the sobering terms and conditions of that covenant. We are to magnify our callings in the priesthood, beware concerning ourselves, give diligent heed to the words of eternal life, and live by every word of God. If we are true to our promises, our part of the covenant, God promises that he will sanctify and renew us and that we will receive all the Father has, which is to say, we will enjoy exaltation in the celestial kingdom with our families forever (D&C 88:33–44). If we are in the line of our duty, if we have pointed ourselves toward eternal life and are striving to keep our temple covenants, we are in line for the highest of eternal rewards. What is required is for us to "be loyal to the royal within us."[6]

Chapter 15

WARS AND RUMORS OF WARS

*W*ar, it seems, is forever with us. Indeed, historians acknowledge that since the 1860s there has not been a time when war of some sort was not underway on this earth. That war comes upon us because of human selfishness is clear from scripture (James 4:1–3, 5–6). The spread of organized conflict is thus an indication of fallen man's having yielded to his own carnal nature and to his basest desires.

Because war will be with us until the King of kings comes to earth to settle all disputes and bring peace, we would be well advised to learn how to deal with the existence of war most productively and positively. Using the Book of Mormon as our guide, let us consider the following suggestions:

1. *Understand what war really is.* "War is basically selfish," President David O. McKay stated. "Its roots feed in the soil of envy, hatred, desire for domination. Its fruit, therefore, is always bitter. . . . The gospel of Jesus Christ is the gospel of peace. . . . There are, however, two conditions which may justify a truly Christian man to enter—mind you, I say *enter, not begin*—a war: (1) An attempt to dominate and to deprive another of his free agency, and, (2) Loyalty to his country. Possibly there is a third,

viz., Defense of a weak nation that is being unjustly crushed by a strong, ruthless one. . . .

"To deprive an intelligent human being of his free agency is to commit the crime of the ages. . . .

"So fundamental in man's eternal progress is his inherent right to choose, that the Lord would defend it even at the price of war. Without freedom of thought, freedom of choice, freedom of action within lawful bounds, man cannot progress."[1]

It was in that spirit, in fact, that the righteous Nephite military leaders led their people into war. First of all, they entered war to protect their families and their civil and religious liberties, feeling that this was an obligation they owed to God as well as their people. Theirs was never an offensive war; they understood that offensive war would bar them from obtaining the blessings of heaven on that kind of war (Alma 43:9–10, 44–47; 48:14–15; 3 Nephi 3:20–21; compare D&C 98:23–36).

2. *Be supportive of constituted government.* In our day the Lord has instructed us that we are to be subject to the government of whatever nation we live in until Christ reigns as King of kings (D&C 58:21–22; 134:1, 5). By means of the title of liberty, Captain Moroni single-handedly sought to foster enthusiasm and engender support for the government by reminding the people of their promises to God (Alma 46). That incident was more than a large pep rally, more than an emotional appeal; it was a covenant-renewal ceremony in which this mighty prophet-leader called upon the people to remember their duty to God, their duty to the Church, their duty to their country, and their duty to one another as Christians. Consequently, we pray earnestly for those who represent us in government and take seriously our own responsibilities as citizens.

3. *Be faithful. Righteousness in society is fundamental.* For the

faithful Nephites, righteousness was at the heart of good government—a government was only as good as its people and its leaders. The Nephites were convinced that they could enjoy the blessings and protection of the Almighty only when they were faithfully keeping their covenants (Alma 46:22). In our day and through the Prophet Joseph Smith, we learn: "I, the Lord God, make you free, therefore ye are free indeed; and the law also maketh you free. Nevertheless, when the wicked rule the people mourn. Wherefore, honest men and wise men should be sought for diligently, and good men and wise men ye should observe to uphold" (D&C 98:8–10).

In speaking of America, Moroni observed, "Behold, this is a choice land, and whatsoever nation shall possess it shall be free from bondage, and from captivity, and from all other nations under heaven, if they will but serve the God of the land, who is Jesus Christ" (Ether 2:12). This is why, no matter how much we might make our influence for good felt in society, the most fundamental and enduring difference we can make in the world is to preach the principles of the restored gospel. Having given high praise to Captain Moroni, Mormon added this important detail, a powerful statement about what good people can and should do during times of war: "Now behold, Helaman and his brethren were no less serviceable unto the people than was Moroni; for they did preach the word of God, and they did baptize unto repentance all men whosoever would hearken unto their words" (Alma 48:19). Indeed, as Alma noted, the preaching of the word has "a great tendency to lead the people to do that which [is] just." In fact, it has a more powerful and far-reaching effect "than the sword, or anything else" (Alma 31:5).

4. *Be positive. Be optimistic. Our circumstances and surroundings need not determine our behavior or our attitude toward daily life.*

We need not be a Pollyanna to be optimistic about living in difficult times. Rather, we need simply to realize that moaning and complaining about the evil of our day will do little to improve the world.

Remarkably good things can and do take place during times of crisis. It was during the period of wars that Alma was taken from the midst of the people, presumably translated and taken from the earth without tasting death (Alma 45:8–19). Mormon writes of a time during the days of the Nephite wars when, because of the steadiness of the members of the Church, "they did prosper exceedingly, and they became exceedingly rich; yea, and they did multiply and wax strong in the land. And thus we see how merciful and just are all the dealings of the Lord, to the fulfilling of all his words unto the children of men. . . . [B]ehold, there never was a happier time among the people of Nephi, since the days of Nephi, than in the days of Moroni" (Alma 50:18–23).

Indeed, the Nephite record provides a profound lesson about how we should respond to our own circumstances: "Thus ended the thirty and first year of the reign of the judges over the people of Nephi; and thus they had had wars, and bloodsheds, and famine, and affliction, for the space of many years. And there had been murders, and contentions, and dissensions, and all manner of iniquity among the people of Nephi; nevertheless for the righteous' sake, yea, because of the prayers of the righteous, they were spared. But behold, because of the exceedingly great length of the war between the Nephites and the Lamanites many had become hardened . . . and many were softened because of their afflictions, insomuch that they did humble themselves before God, even in the depth of humility" (Alma 62:39–41). How individuals reacted to pain, to distress, to heartache, to strife in society was a personal choice.

A bit of perspective on the future may be helpful. Although we know that wars and bloodshed and gross wickedness will characterize much of the planet until the beginning of the millennial reign, we also know that consummate righteousness and peace will be found among the Saints of the Most High. That is, while the mother of abominations spreads her nefarious influence throughout the four corners of the earth, the Church of the Lamb will spread a righteous influence, albeit on a smaller scale. "And it came to pass that I, Nephi, beheld the power of the Lamb of God, that it descended upon the saints of the church of the Lamb, and upon the covenant people of the Lord, who were scattered upon all the face of the earth; and they were armed with righteousness and with the power of God in great glory" (1 Nephi 14:14).

While tears and tests and trials lie ahead, there is so very much to look forward to: the spread of the restored gospel to all the world, temples dotting the earth, Latter-day Saints providing a leavening influence in the arts, sciences, education, and entertainment. There is so much for us to have faith in, not the least of which is the future of the United States of America. "Men may fail in this country," President Harold B. Lee affirmed to Ricks College students in 1973, "earthquakes may come, seas may heave beyond their bounds, there may be great drought, disaster, and hardship, but *this nation, founded on principles laid down by men whom God raised up, will never fail. This is the cradle of humanity, . . . the place of the new Jerusalem. . . . I have faith in America; you and I must have faith in America, if we understand the teachings of the gospel of Jesus Christ. . . .*

"I plead with you not to preach pessimism. Preach that this is the greatest country in all the world. This is the favored land. This is the land of our forefathers. It is the nation that will stand despite whatever trials or crises it may yet have to pass through."[2]

A passage of scripture that has special appeal to me is from the writings of the apostle Paul: "Whatsoever things are true, whatsoever things are honest, whatsoever things are just, whatsoever things are pure, whatsoever things are lovely, whatsoever things are of good report; if there be any virtue, and if there be any praise, think on these things" (Philippians 4:8; emphasis added). Paul tells us that we are to focus upon things that are true, honest, just, pure, lovely, of good report, virtuous, and praiseworthy. While we are not to be naïve in regard to evil or foolish in regard to unholy influences about us, we are not to fixate upon them or conclude that all is lost. There is too much good to be seen and acknowledged, too much good to be enjoyed and appreciated, too much good to be accomplished by those intent on the salvation of souls. We have no time for despair, no time for feeling sorry for ourselves; we have time only to be about our Father's business.

Chapter 16

THE FALL OF BABYLON

As we move toward the Millennium, we can anticipate a growing polarization between good and evil. Surely there will be fewer and fewer lukewarm Latter-day Saints as time passes and more of those who either commit themselves fully to building God's kingdom or who oppose outright that which they once embraced. Near the close of his second book, Nephi, son of Lehi, wrote: "And it shall come to pass that the Lord God shall commence his work among all nations, kindreds, tongues, and people, to bring about the restoration of his people upon the earth. And with righteousness shall the Lord God judge the poor, and reprove with equity for the meek of the earth. And he shall smite the earth with the rod of his mouth; and with the breath of his lips shall he slay the wicked. For the time speedily cometh that the Lord God shall cause *a great division among the people*, and the wicked will he destroy; and he will spare his people, yea, even if it so be that he must destroy the wicked by fire" (2 Nephi 30:8–10; emphasis added).

In modern revelation we read: "And until that hour [the coming of the Son of Man] there will be foolish virgins among the wise; and at that hour cometh *an entire separation of the righteous and the wicked*; and in that day will I send mine angels to pluck out the wicked and cast them into unquenchable fire" (D&C 63:54; emphasis added). Righteousness will flourish, and wickedness will spread. In other words, the good among men and women will get better, while the evil will ripen in iniquity. Zion will fill the earth, as will Babylon; consummate righteousness will be opposed by a strangling and stultifying wickedness.

Quite early in the Book of Mormon we are introduced to what is called the great and abominable church, the mother of abominations, the whore of all the earth. Who or what is this? Jacob explains that "he that fighteth against Zion, both Jew and Gentile, both bond and free, both male and female, shall perish; for they are they who are the whore of all the earth; for they who are not for me are against me, saith our God" (2 Nephi 10:16).

Elder B. H. Roberts put it this way: "I understand the injunction to Oliver Cowdery to 'contend against no church, save it be the church of the devil' (D&C 18:20), to mean that he shall contend against evil, against untruth, against all combinations of wicked men. They constitute the church of the devil, the kingdom of evil, a federation of unrighteousness; and the servants of God have a right to contend against that which is evil, let it appear where it will. . . . [O]ur relationship to the religious world is not one that calls for the denunciation of sectarian churches as composing the church of the devil. All that makes for untruth, for unrighteousness constitutes the kingdom of evil—the church of the devil." Now note the kind of breadth necessary in reaching out and understanding our brothers and sisters of other faiths. Elder Roberts continued: "All that makes for truth, for righteousness, is of God; it constitutes the kingdom of righteousness—the empire of Jehovah; and, in a certain sense at least, constitutes the Church of Christ. With the latter—the kingdom of righteousness—we have no warfare. On the contrary both the spirit of the Lord's commandments to His servants and the dictates of right reason would suggest that we seek to enlarge this kingdom of righteousness both by recognizing such truths as it possesses and seeking the friendship and co-operation of the righteous men and women who constitute its membership."[1]

As Zion is the counterpart to Babylon, so the Church of Jesus Christ is the counterpart to the church of the devil. In one of the most fascinating and hopeful descriptions of the very last days, Nephi records: "And it came to pass that I looked and beheld the whore of all the earth, and *she sat upon many waters*" (1 Nephi 14:11). John the Revelator, who may well have seen the same vision Nephi saw, recorded that "the waters which thou sawest, where the whore sitteth, are peoples, and multitudes, and nations, and tongues" (Revelation 17:15).

Nephi continued: "And she [the mother of harlots] had dominion over all the earth, among all nations, kindreds, tongues, and people." Now notice what Nephi says about its counterpart: "And it came to pass that I beheld the church of the Lamb of God, and its numbers were few, because of the wickedness and abominations of the whore who sat upon many waters; nevertheless, I beheld that *the church of the Lamb, who were the saints of God, were also upon all the face of the earth* (1 Nephi 14:11–12; emphasis added).

Let us be clear that the war against the great and abominable church will not be won through hand-to-hand combat, sea-to-air missiles, or nuclear devices. Victory will come because the power of God will descend upon the covenant people of the Lord; these people will be armed with righteousness and the power of God. If we keep in mind that the great and abominable church is any organization—social, economic, political, fraternal, philosophical, or religious—that fights against the establishment of the kingdom of God, then we will realize that in that future day the Saints will not simply be about the business of denouncing false doctrines or corrupted ordinances, although there will surely be much of that. The Saints will be persons of honesty and integrity, men and women of conscience and sensitivity who stand up and speak out against man's inhumanity to man; against deceit and dishonesty in business practices; against the proliferation of immorality and violence in real life as well as in virtual reality on the Internet, on the stage and screen, and on television. As we approach the end of the world, which is the destruction of the wicked (Joseph Smith–Matthew 1:4, 31), we can expect to witness the collapse of one corrupt organization after another, which have become havens for pride and arrogance and greed. We can expect to watch as the shallowness and superficiality of the worldly wise, those who have read by the lamp of their own conceit, is exposed.

We read in the Apocalypse: "And after these things I saw another angel come down from heaven, having great power; and the earth was lightened with his glory. And he cried mightily with a strong voice, saying, Babylon the great is fallen, is fallen. . . . And I heard another voice from heaven, saying, Come out of her, my people, that ye be not partakers of her sins, and that ye receive not of her plagues. For her sins have reached unto heaven, and God hath remembered her iniquities" (Revelation 18:1–5).

Nephi explained that "the blood of that great and abominable church, which is the whore of all the earth, shall turn upon their own heads; for they shall war among themselves, and the sword of their own hands shall fall upon their own heads, and they shall be drunken with their own blood. And every nation which shall war against thee, O house of Israel, shall be turned one against another, and they shall fall into the pit which they digged to ensnare the people of the Lord. And all that fight against Zion shall be destroyed, and that great whore, who hath perverted the right ways of the Lord, yea, that great and abominable church, shall tumble to the dust and great shall be the fall of it" (1 Nephi 22:13–14; see also verse 23).

One day things will change. The lowly will be exalted. The unpretentious and the spontaneously (but silent) righteous men and women will be acknowledged from the housetops. Malice and malevolence will melt away as the hoar frost, while benevolence and beneficence will become the order of the day. President Howard W. Hunter testified: "In a world too preoccupied with winning through intimidation and seeking to be number one, no large crowd of folk is standing in line to buy books that call for mere meekness. But *the meek shall inherit the earth, a pretty impressive corporate takeover—and done* without *intimidation*! Sooner or later, and we pray sooner *than* later, everyone will acknowledge that Christ's way is not only the *right* way, but ultimately the *only* way to hope and joy. Every knee shall bow and every tongue will confess that *gentleness is better than brutality, that kindness is greater than coercion, that the soft voice turneth away wrath.* In the end, and sooner than that whenever possible, we must be more like him."[2] We as Latter-day Saints help to prepare the earth for the second coming of Christ as we prepare ourselves to be clean and competent vessels in the hands of the Lord, as we keep ourselves "on the Lord's side of the line,"[3] and as we cultivate and celebrate the gift of the Holy Ghost. Out of such a life peace, perspective, and joy come.

Chapter 17

"MY PEOPLE WILL I PRESERVE"

My wife and I attended a funeral not long ago for a very fine Latter-day Saint man—a devoted husband, loving father, and a great Christian in his community. Tributes were paid to him by many of his friends and priesthood leaders; we learned that he was not only extremely helpful to people in the neighborhood but also quite a comedian. A good man, a fun personality, to be sure. There were many well-wishers and persons who assured the man's wife that they would be available if she needed to talk and close at hand when she felt especially lonely. Like most Latter-day Saint funerals, it was in a sense a happy occasion, a celebration of a great life, a tribute to a superb human being. And yet I noticed the genuine pain and sense of loss and separation in his wife's countenance and observed the shock and trauma in the faces of the children. Their father was gone, and he was taken from them at only fifty-nine years of age.

I was reminded of an important principle on that day: even though the teachings of the restored gospel bring peace and a marvelous perspective on life and death, and though the knowledge of the plan of salvation may prevent us from grieving as do those who have no hope (1 Thessalonians 4:13), the gospel does not really remove the anguish of loss and separation that the sweet mother and adoring children will know in the weeks and months and years to come. Death is painful, even for those who are living the gospel. To be completely honest, I am not afraid of death; it's the dying part that worries me. It's the getting to death that makes me just a bit nervous.

To some extent, it is the same with the events that lie ahead, events that are a significant part of the signs of the times. We may be living in such a manner as to buffer ourselves somewhat from the sober realities and stark episodes that will yet be visited upon this planet, but that does not prevent us from feeling some apprehension. How could we be completely unmoved or unflappable in the midst of natural disasters, death and diseases, plagues, wars, astral phenomena, or signs in the heavens? What should be our approach to life here and now when we read that "a desolating scourge shall go forth among the inhabitants of the earth, and shall continue to be poured out from time to time, if they repent not, until the earth is empty, and the inhabitants thereof are consumed away and utterly destroyed by the brightness of my coming"? (D&C 5:19).

How are we to respond to such prophecies as this one? "Wherefore, I the Lord God will send forth flies upon the face of the earth, which shall take hold of the inhabitants thereof, and shall eat their flesh, and shall cause maggots to come in upon them; and their tongues shall be stayed that they shall not utter against me; and their flesh shall fall from off their bones, and their eyes from their sockets; and it shall come to pass that the beasts of the forest and the fowls of the air shall devour them up"? (D&C 29:18–20). Such scriptural passages may cause even the most seasoned student of scripture to fear and tremble.

Is there no hope? Is there no deliverance? Is there nothing

that can be done to avoid all of those and ten thousand other prophesied plights that are to come upon the children of God?

Of course there is. If we can purify our lives and bring about a worldwide conversion of souls, a wholesale repentance of the inhabitants of the planet, then many if not most of these cataclysms can be averted. The Church of Jesus Christ will continue to cry repentance unto this generation, to lift the warning voice, and to seek to prepare the people for the second coming of the Savior. We must be positive, must assume a wholesome and affirmative stance toward national and world conditions, and must do everything in our power to love the children of God and work for their best good.

But in the end what will be, will be. The prophetic picture does not suggest that the world will get better, that everyone will suddenly (or even gradually) begin to keep the commandments and apply the teachings of Jesus, or that most of the people on the planet will eventually be prepared to receive their returning King. How then shall we live? Is there any benefit to living the gospel if in fact the world will be destroyed?

Of course there is. Those who align themselves with the word and will of the Almighty will enjoy the comfort and consolation and direction of the Holy Spirit. But will all of the faithful be spared and saved from the coming days of desolation?

We learn from the Prophet Joseph Smith's inspired translation of the early chapters of Genesis about the great antediluvian prophet and seer Enoch. In vision Enoch was permitted to see the future—the translation of his own City of Holiness, as well as the days of wickedness and vengeance in the time of Noah. In addition, he was allowed to look ahead, down through the corridors of time.

"And the Lord said unto Enoch: As I live, even so will I come in the last days, in the days of wickedness and vengeance, to ful-fill the oath which I have made unto you concerning the children of Noah; and the day shall come that the earth shall rest [the Millennium], but before that day the heavens shall be darkened, and a veil of darkness shall cover the earth; and the heavens shall shake, and also the earth; and *great tribulations shall be among the children of men, but my people will I preserve*" (Moses 7:60–61; em-phasis added).

Latter-day revelation and modern prophets have repeatedly taught that there is safety in the stakes of Zion, meaning, within the Church, through the teachings of the restored gospel, and by obedience to the commandments of God: "Verily I say unto you all: Arise and shine forth, that thy light may be a standard for the nations; and that *the gathering together upon the land of Zion, and upon her stakes,* may be for a defense, and for a refuge from the storm, and from wrath *when it shall be poured out without mixture upon the whole earth*" (D&C 115:5–6; emphasis added).

Joseph Smith put it this way: "There will be here and there a Stake [of Zion] for the gathering of the Saints. Some may have cried peace, but the Saints and the world will have little peace from henceforth. Let this not hinder us from going to the Stakes. . . . There your children shall be blessed, and you in the midst of friends where you may be blessed. The Gospel net gathers of every kind." The Prophet said further, "The time is soon coming, when no man will have any peace but in Zion and her stakes."[1]

Surely personal righteousness will keep us from Satan's power and prevent the enemy of all righteousness from gaining a foot-hold in our lives and in our homes. In that sense, all who stay on the gospel path will know the protection that comes only through faithfulness. The Prophet Joseph explained that "it is a false idea that the Saints will escape all the judgments, whilst the wicked suffer; for all flesh is subject to suffer, and 'the righteous shall hardly escape'; still many of the Saints will escape, for the just shall live by faith; yet many of the righteous shall fall a prey to disease, to pestilence, etc., by reason of the weakness of the flesh, and yet be saved in the Kingdom of God. So that it is an unhallowed principle to say that such and such have transgressed because they have been preyed upon by disease or death, for all flesh is subject to death; and the Savior has said, 'Judge not, lest ye be judged.'"[2]

In speaking at a general welfare meeting of the Church, Elder Bruce R. McConkie said: "We do not know when the calamities and troubles of the last days will fall upon any of us as individuals or upon bodies of the Saints. The Lord deliberately withholds from us the day and hour of his coming and of the tribulations which shall precede it—all as part of the testing and probationary experiences of mortality. He simply tells us to watch and be ready.

"We can rest assured that if we have done all in our power to prepare for whatever lies ahead, he will then help us with whatever else we need. . . .

"We do not say that all of the Saints will be spared and saved from the coming day of desolation. But we do say there is no promise of safety and no promise of security except for those who love the Lord and who are seeking to do all that he commands.

"It may be, for instance, that nothing except the power of faith and the authority of the priesthood can save individuals and congregations from the atomic holocausts that surely shall be.

"And so we raise the warning voice and say: Take heed; prepare; watch and be ready. There is no security in any course except the course of obedience and conformity and righteousness."[3]

Those of us who have received the restored gospel are called upon to be people who are different in a world spiraling toward

Sodom. Our warning voice may well be sounded just as loudly by how we live as by what we say. We sound our voices when we discipline ourselves to avoid the allurements of Babylon, when we make a decision as sons and daughters of God to stand, with our families and our congregations, as stark contrasts to the shoddy and superficial deeds of the sons and daughters of men. And yet we are called to stand up, to be willing to identify evil for what it is, and to celebrate goodness wherever it may be found. We are charged to expose clever and costly compromise as well as to hold tenaciously to those absolute truths and eternal values that have been the foundation stones of civilizations from the beginning. In short, the disciples of Jesus Christ are commissioned to be the salt of the earth, the lasting leavening influence that will preserve a people and promote a divine cause.

Chapter 18

THE NEW JERUSALEM

$\mathcal{F}$or millennia, Christians have been obsessed with the establishment of what St. Augustine called the City of God, a place of spiritual refuge, a holy commonwealth, even a paradise on earth. Yes, earnest and God-fearing people have concerned themselves principally with personal purity and individual salvation, but true disciples of the Lord Jesus Christ have longed for the time when the good news of the gospel could be incorporated into society, when fear and hate and greed would be done away. They have yearned for the day when earth's inhabitants would put their "trust in that Spirit which leadeth to do good—yea, to do justly, to walk humbly, to judge righteously" (D&C 11:12).

We cannot grow in those spiritual graces that qualify us for eternal life by living in isolation; the deepest and most profound enjoyments of Christianity are to be found only in community. As the Prophet Joseph Smith explained, "The greatest temporal and spiritual blessings which always come from faithfulness and concerted effort, never attended individual exertion or enterprise. The history of all past ages abundantly attests this fact."[1]

What is the origin for such strivings for sociality? It may well be that deep within the soul of every son and daughter of God is the distant memory that we once lived in the family order, that each one of us "is a beloved spirit son or daughter of heavenly parents, and, as such, each has a divine nature and destiny."[2]

In addition, holy scripture attests that several millennia ago men and women were able, through applying the principles of the holy gospel, to establish heaven on earth and to pull down from the heavens unspeakable blessings upon the heads of earth's inhabitants. Moses recorded the following cryptic verse: "And Enoch walked with God: and he was not; for God took him" (Genesis 5:24).

The apostle Paul was a bit more detailed in his description of Enoch the antediluvian: "By faith Enoch was translated that he should not see death; and was not found, because God had translated him: for before his translation he had this testimony, that he pleased God" (Hebrews 11:5). It is of course to latter-day revelation that we turn to discover one of earth's grand success stories—the spiritual transformation of an entire society. It is in Joseph Smith's marvelous new translation of the King James Bible that we encounter, in astonishing detail, the life and ministry of Enoch, that stammering and stuttering youth called by God to cry repentance to a people steeped in iniquity, that hesitant but heroic young man whose very name is today associated with transcendent righteousness.

As a result of Enoch's tenacity, his refusal to yield to feelings of inadequacy, and his implicit trust in the Word, he became a powerful instrument in the hands of Jehovah to create the ancient Zion. "And the Lord called his people Zion, because they were of one heart and one mind, and dwelt in righteousness; and there was no poor among them" (Moses 7:18). Zion, glorious Zion, the people of promise and the place of the pure in heart (D&C 97:21).

Enoch's Zion was taken from the earth and the people were

translated. Enoch's Zion became the model, the type after which subsequent generations of prophets and peoples sought to pattern themselves (JST, Genesis 14:25–40). Like Abraham, the ancients "looked for a city which hath foundations, whose builder and maker is God" (Hebrews 11:10). Enoch's Zion became for Joseph Smith the scriptural prototype, the ancient model for a modern City of Holiness. He taught that "we ought to have the building up of Zion as our greatest object."[3] And so it is that Zion has been established whenever and wherever members of the Church of Jesus Christ have settled and where the principles and ordinances of the gospel are incorporated.

Early in the dispensation of the fulness of times, the Lord informed his Seer and the people of covenant that the site of what he called the New Jerusalem would soon be given (D&C 28:9; 42:9, 35, 62). The New Jerusalem was to be, as its ancient namesake had been centuries before, a holy land, an abode of the prophets and seers, a place from which the word of the Lord would be sounded and would go forth to all the world. In 1831 the Lord revealed that the center place of Zion, the New Jerusalem, was Independence, Jackson County, Missouri (D&C 57:3). As time passed and as the Latter-day Saints matured spiritually, the Prophet Joseph began to point out that although there was to be a center place, a central site (Jackson County, Missouri), the tent of Zion was to spread and expand, even as Isaiah had foretold (Isaiah 54; D&C 82:14). In that sense, each stake was to become the center place of Zion for its people, its own little New Jerusalem. So while "Zion (the New Jerusalem) will be built upon the American continent" (Articles of Faith 1:10), "*so also shall there be Zions in all lands and New Jerusalems in the mountains of the Lord in all the earth*. But the American Zion shall be the capital city, the source whence the law shall go forth to govern all the earth. It shall be the city of the Great King. His throne shall be there, and from there he shall reign gloriously over all the earth."[4]

In his abridgment of the Jaredite record, Moroni spoke of the wickedness of the Jaredites: "For behold, they rejected all the words of Ether; for he truly told them of all things, from the beginning of man; and that after the waters had receded from off the face of this land [the flood in the days of Noah] it became a choice land above all other lands, a chosen land of the Lord; wherefore the Lord would have that all men should serve him who dwell upon the face thereof; and that it was the place of the New Jerusalem, which should come down out of heaven, and the holy sanctuary of the Lord. Behold, Ether saw the days of Christ, and he spake concerning a New Jerusalem upon this land." And what kind of people were to be found in this New Jerusalem? Ether declared that "blessed are they who dwell therein, for it is they whose garments are white through the blood of the Lamb" (Ether 13:2–4, 10).

We are comforted to know that Enoch preserved his people during a time of great wickedness and vengeance. Enoch's account continues: "*And righteousness will I send down out of heaven; and truth will I send forth out of the earth,* to bear testimony of mine Only Begotten; his resurrection from the dead; yea, and also the resurrection of all men; and *righteousness and truth will I cause to sweep the earth as with a flood,* to gather out mine elect from the four quarters of the earth, unto a place which I shall prepare, an Holy City, that my people may gird up their loins, and be looking forth for the time of my coming; for there shall be my tabernacle, and it shall be called Zion, a New Jerusalem.

"And the Lord said unto Enoch: Then shalt thou and all thy city meet them [Zion on earth] there, and we will receive them into our bosom, and they shall see us; and we will fall upon their necks, and they shall fall upon our necks, and we will kiss each other; and there shall be mine abode, and it shall be Zion, . . . and for the space of a thousand years the earth shall rest" (Moses 7:62–64; emphasis added).

Beginning in the spring of 1820, righteousness and truth did indeed begin to be sent forth from the heavens: the transcendent appearance of the Father and the Son, followed by a whole host of angelic ministrants, initiated this final dispensation of grace. Truth did spring forth out of the earth: the stick of Joseph spoke of an American branch of Hebrews and bore testimony of the divine Sonship of Christ, of his atoning sacrifice and resurrection, and of the coming resurrection of all those who had taken a physical body. And the Book of Mormon would be the great instrument of gathering Israel in the last days into those cities of holiness we know as Zion, the New Jerusalem. What a glorious day it will be! Zion from above, the city of Enoch, will join and unite with Zion from below, which is the members of the Church of Jesus Christ who have prepared themselves for this grand reunion.

Both Enoch and Noah were given a sign from God—a rainbow. As every Primary child has learned, the rainbow would stand as a reminder that the God of heaven would never again flood the earth by water. There was, however, a more subtle but powerful message that was to surge through the minds of Noah's descendants when they beheld the rainbow in the sky: they were reminded that when in the last days the people of Zion found themselves looking to the heavens more earnestly; when they found themselves yearning for that supernal reunion of the cities of holiness, they were to be assured that Zion from above was in fact looking down upon them. "And *the general assembly of the church of the first-born shall come down out of heaven, and possess the earth,* and shall have place until the end come. And this is mine everlasting covenant, which I made with thy father Enoch" (JST, Genesis 9:23;

emphasis added). The Church of the Firstborn, the inner Church, the Church within the veil, the Church made up of those who will be exalted and live forevermore in the highest degree of the celestial kingdom—that body of believers would be established on an earth that would, after a thousand years of millennial splendor, receive its final sanctification and become the eternal abode of God and those who have been "made perfect through Jesus the mediator of the new covenant, who wrought out this perfect atonement through the shedding of his own blood" (D&C 76:69).

And what part shall we play in this grand drama? Simply stated, we can strive now to establish Zion—in our personal lives, in our homes, in our social relations, in our community and our world. We can labor diligently to see that there is no poor among us—no poor economically, emotionally, intellectually. We can be an example of the believers (1 Timothy 4:12), an illustration of the difference the gospel of Jesus Christ and the priesthood of Almighty God can make in the lives of men and women. We can be bolder than we are now in declaring the message of the Restoration; we can do our part to "flood the earth with the Book of Mormon."[5]

"And now, I ask," Joseph Smith inquired, "how righteousness and truth are going to sweep the earth as with a flood? I will answer. *Men and angels are to be co-workers in bringing to pass this great work, and Zion is to be prepared, even a New Jerusalem,* for the elect that are to be gathered from the four quarters of the earth, and to be established an holy city, for the tabernacle of the Lord shall be with them."[6]

What we do to further the work of God's kingdom within our own geography will prove to be a significant part of the establishment of a worldwide Zion.

Chapter 19

KNOWING THE
SIGNS OF THE TIMES

During the early 1970s there was much in the media about how the people of the United States could "prepare for the coming crash." There was much tension, uncertainty, and fear about what was in the offing. Would the imminent financial crisis spell the end of American culture as we knew it? Were we, as some religionists contended, approaching the end of the world? Would we soon see the pestilence and plague and tribulations of which the prophets had spoken? Was the second coming of Jesus Christ just around the corner? Were we out of time?

In the midst of this furor, a modern prophet spoke out. President Harold B. Lee raised a warning voice: "There are among us many loose writings predicting the calamities which are about to overtake us. Some of these have been publicized as though they were necessary to wake up the world to the horrors about to overtake us. Many of these are from sources upon which there cannot be unquestioned reliance.

"Are you . . . aware of the fact that we need no such publications to be forewarned, if we were only conversant with what the scriptures have already spoken to us in plainness?

"Let me give you the sure word of prophecy on which you

should rely for your guide instead of these strange sources which may have great political implications.

"Read the 24th chapter of Matthew—particularly that inspired version as contained in the Pearl of Great Price [Joseph Smith–Matthew].

"Then read the 45th section of the Doctrine and Covenants where the Lord, not man, has documented the signs of the times.

"Now turn to section 101 and section 133 of the Doctrine and Covenants and hear the step-by-step recounting of events leading up to the coming of the Savior.

"Finally, turn to the promises the Lord makes to those who keep the commandments when these judgments descend upon the wicked, as set forth in the Doctrine and Covenants, section 38.

" . . . [T]hese are some of the writings with which you should concern yourselves, rather than commentaries that may come from those whose information may not be the most reliable and whose motives may be subject to question."[1]

I was in the Salt Lake Tabernacle when President Lee sounded those warnings; I felt the power of God's Spirit as it was poured out upon the congregation. The Holy Spirit of God affirmed that what the living oracle had just spoken was true and from God. I left the Tabernacle with a number of resolutions in my mind and heart—and those resolutions have never left me—that I would keep my eyes on those whom we sustain as prophets, seers, and revelators; that I would attend especially to what they had to say relative to the world in which we live; that I would study and ponder and cross-reference their messages into my scriptures; and that I would use the words of the apostles and prophets as the standard against which I would assess the accuracy and reliability of the unreliable trumpets in society. Keeping these resolutions has been a rich blessing.

In the process I have gleaned a few principles relative to reading the signs of the times. I do not have authority to speak for the Church, so I cannot "write by way of commandment, but by wisdom" (D&C 28:5). I have sought, nevertheless, to do so in harmony with the teachings of modern prophets. Consider the following ideas, which I hope will be helpful to you.

1. When the Savior says, "I come quickly," which he does many times, both in the Bible (Revelation 22:20) and especially in modern revelation (D&C 33:18; 34:12; 35:27; 39:24; 41:4; 49:28; 51:20; 54:10; 68:35; 88:126; 99:5; 112:34), he does not mean he is coming at any moment; rather, the Savior will come suddenly, unannounced. It is the Lord's call to spiritual vigilance.

2. It is simply impossible to tie down every prophecy, to link each one completely with similar ones, and to construct a chronological chart of the signs of the times. As Elder Bruce R. McConkie put it: "It is not always possible for us in our present state of spiritual enlightenment to put every event into an exact category or time frame. We are left to ponder and wonder about many things, perhaps to keep us alert and attentive to the commandments should the Lord come in our day. And some of the prophetic utterances apply to both pre- and post-millennial events; some have an initial and partial fulfillment in our day and shall have a second and grander completion in the days ahead."[2] We must be especially careful, for example, in how we interpret such terms as "then" or "in that day," words used quite often in referring to the future.

3. It is often difficult to discern between when the prophetic word is to be understood literally and when the Lord and his prophets choose to speak in metaphor, allegory, or in beautiful symbolism. It is only by the power of the Spirit—the same Spirit

that attended the prophets—that we are enabled to "rightly divid[e] the word of truth" (2 Timothy 2:15).

4. In a revelation given through Joseph Smith to Orson Hyde, Luke S. Johnson, Lyman E. Johnson, and William E. McLellin, men who would be called to the first Quorum of the Twelve Apostles in this dispensation, we read the following: "And unto you it shall be given to know the signs of the times, and the signs of the coming of the Son of Man" (D&C 68:11). Although each disciple of Christ should seek the spirit of prophecy and revelation and strive to understand the signs of the times, we would be especially wise to heed the statements of those charged to guide the destiny of God's Church and kingdom.

Elder M. Russell Ballard of the Quorum of the Twelve Apostles offered the following timely advice to Brigham Young University students: "I am called as one of the apostles to be a special witness of Christ in these exciting, trying times, and I do not know when He is going to come again. As far as I know, none of my brethren in the Council of the Twelve or even in the First Presidency know. And I would humbly suggest to you, my young brothers and sisters, that *if we do not know, then nobody knows,* no matter how compelling their arguments or how reasonable their calculations. . . .

"I believe when the Lord says 'no man' knows, it really means that no man knows. You should be extremely wary of anyone who claims to be an exception to divine decree."[3]

5. We are wise to spend the greater portion of our time and energy with the scriptures of the Restoration. It interests me that in his warnings about "loose writings," President Harold B. Lee instructed the Saints to do that very thing—spend time with the scriptures of the Restoration. He did not refer Church members to Isaiah or Ezekiel or Daniel or Revelation. Nearly a decade

later, President Marion G. Romney elaborated: "In each dispensation, . . . the Lord has revealed anew the principles of the gospel. So that while the records of past dispensations, insofar as they are uncorrupted, testify to the truths of the gospel, still each dispensation has had revealed in its day sufficient truth to guide the people of the new dispensation, independent of the records of the past.

"I do not wish to discredit in any manner the records we have of the truths revealed by the Lord in past dispensations. What I now desire is to impress upon our minds that *the gospel, as revealed to the Prophet Joseph Smith, is complete and is the word direct from heaven to this dispensation. It alone is sufficient to teach us the principles of eternal life. It is the truth revealed, the commandments given in this dispensation through modern prophets by which we are to be governed.*"[4]

6. In addition to focusing on modern revelation, we should be especially attentive to the words of those apostles and prophets charged to lead the Church *in our day*. Elder Jeffrey R. Holland put it this way: "We believe in a God who is engaged in our lives, who is not silent, not absent. . . . In this Church, even our young Primary children recite, 'We believe all that God has revealed, all that He does now reveal, and we believe that He will yet reveal many great and important things pertaining to the Kingdom of God.' (Articles of Faith 1:9).

"In declaring new scripture and continuing revelation, we pray we will never be arrogant or insensitive. But after a sacred vision in a now sacred grove answered in the affirmative the question 'Does God exist?' what Joseph Smith and The Church of Jesus Christ of Latter-day Saints force us to face is the next interrogative, which necessarily follows: 'Does He speak?' . . .

"In a sense Joseph Smith and his prophetic successors in this

Church answer the challenge Ralph Waldo Emerson put to the students of the Harvard Divinity School [175] years ago. . . . To that group of the Protestant best and brightest, the great sage of Concord pled that they teach 'that God is, not was; that He speaketh, not spake.'"[5]

7. Stay in the mainstream of the Church. Never try to be truer than true. Avoid the kind of excessive zeal that results in spiritual imbalance and instability. Live a balanced life. Devote time occasionally to a study of the signs of the times, but study widely and study the whole gospel; do not allow your search of the revelations concerning the last days to become a gospel hobby.[6] Specialize in the fundamentals, and find delight in the first principles and ordinances of the gospel. Serious students of scripture will gradually discover a second simplicity, a simplicity beyond complexity.

We are told in the Bible that the Lord Jesus Christ will come "as a thief in the night" (1 Thessalonians 5:2; 2 Peter 3:10; see also Revelation 3:3). That is, he will come suddenly, unexpectedly, when the generality of humankind is unprepared, unready, not watching. For such persons, the Lord's Advent will be an unwelcome event. For far too many, it will be terrible. This need not be the case with the Lord's Saints. Through the Prophet Joseph Smith, the Master clarified: "And again, verily I say unto you, the coming of the Lord draweth nigh, and *it overtaketh the world as a thief in the night*—therefore, gird up your loins, that you may be the children of light, and that day shall not overtake you as a thief" (D&C 106:4–5; emphasis added).

"While we are powerless to alter the fact of the Second Coming and unable to know its exact time," Elder Dallin H. Oaks explained, "we can accelerate our own preparation and try to influence the preparation of those around us." And then, after citing several scriptural warnings, Elder Oaks asked: "What if the day of his coming were tomorrow? If we knew that we would meet the Lord tomorrow—through our premature death or His unexpected coming—what would we do today? What confessions would we make? What practices would we discontinue? What accounts would we settle? What forgivenesses would we extend? What testimonies would we bear?

"If we would do these things then, why not now? Why not seek peace while peace can be obtained? If our lamps of preparation are drawn down, let us start immediately to replenish them."[7]

May we read the signs of the times by the lamp of humility and as guided by the Light of the world.

Chapter 20

MEN AND WOMEN OF DESTINY

As members of The Church of Jesus Christ of Latter-day Saints, we have, as it were, one eye riveted on the present and another focused on the future. While a knowledge of what lies ahead can assist us immeasurably to see things today in perspective, we cannot live in the future; all we have is now.

As to the present, Elder Dallin H. Oaks spoke soberly: "Evil that used to be localized and covered like a boil is now legalized and paraded like a banner. The most fundamental roots and bulwarks of civilization are questioned or attacked. Nations disavow their religious heritage. Marriage and family responsibilities are discarded as impediments to personal indulgence. The movies and magazines and television that shape our attitudes are filled with stories or images that portray the children of God as predatory beasts or, at best, as trivial creations pursuing little more than personal pleasure. And too many of us accept this as entertainment.

"The men and women who made epic sacrifices to combat evil regimes in the past were shaped by values that are disappearing from our public teaching. The good, the true, and the beautiful are being replaced by the no-good, the 'whatever,' and the valueless fodder of personal whim."[1]

Let us now turn our attention to the *personal* responsibilities you and I share as we do our part to prepare the world for the second coming of the Son of God. President Thomas S. Monson has reminded us that "the world is in need of your help. There are feet to steady, hands to grasp, minds to encourage, hearts to inspire, and souls to save. The blessings of eternity await you. Yours is the privilege to be not spectators but participants."[2]

There are indeed *feet to steady*. So many of our Heavenly Father's children trip and stumble over the pebbles and rocks in their path. Some wrestle with fear, others with anxiety or depression. Our settled conviction of the truth, our simple testimony, can be as oil on troubled waters. We need to open our mouths and our hearts. Many of the children of God roam to and fro across the earth in search of fulfillment, of purpose, of direction. The restored gospel is a roadmap to the displaced as well as manna to starving souls. We can offer it to the hungry and the unsettled; we can be assured that it will help profoundly to fill that God-shaped hole in their hearts. We can step up, speak out, and testify by deeds as well as in words. Gospel gladness empowers and sustains our walk with the Lord.

There are *hands to grasp*. Peter grasped the hand of the lame beggar at the Gate Beautiful. By the power of the priesthood and in the name of Jesus Christ he lifted that son of God to his feet (Acts 3:1–10). Peter changed his life. That meridian apostle was able to lift another soul because he stood on higher ground.[3] We can grasp the hands of family members and friends whose lives are steeped in sin and who harbor the false and damning notion that they have placed themselves beyond the reach of God's grace. We can bring resolve into their lives once again by assuring them that "there is never a time when the spirit is too old to approach God. All are within reach of pardoning mercy, who have not committed the unpardonable sin."[4]

There are *minds to encourage*. We can present the message of the restored gospel to a world that is sinking beneath the weight of its own ignorance and uncertainties, a world that yearns for answers to life's most vexing questions. Truly, the principles and doctrines delivered through modern prophets in the dispensation of the fulness of times is as stimulating to the mind as it is soothing and settling to the heart.

There are *hearts to inspire*. The Saints of the Most High have received, as the greatest of all the treasures they hold, the gift of the Holy Ghost,[5] the right to enjoy the close companionship of a member of the Godhead. That Comforter, the Holy Spirit of Promise, is the only true source of solace in a culture gripped by existential anguish. It is by means of this grand bestowal that the pilgrims of planet earth can find delight and say, "God is with us."

There are *souls to save*. Our Father in heaven did not send us to earth to fail. No person came into the second estate who was incapable of gaining the fulness of celestial glory. Joseph Smith challenged a major segment of the religious world in his day that had imbibed the futile and fatalistic concept that only the elect, only those predestined to salvation, would accept the Gospel and come to faith. His simple words offer supernal comfort: "We believe that through the Atonement of Christ, *all mankind may be saved*, by obedience to the laws and ordinances of the Gospel" (Articles of Faith 1:3; emphasis added). "For this is good and acceptable in the sight of God our Saviour; who will have all men to be saved, and to come unto the knowledge of the truth" (1 Timothy 2:3–4). God is longsuffering toward us, "not willing that any should perish, but that all should come to repentance" (2 Peter 3:9).

I am stirred up to remembrance of my duty when I contemplate the words that so affected a young and discouraged missionary, David O. McKay: "Whate'er Thou Art, Act Well Thy Part."[6] The words serve as powerful reminders not only of what we must do but, perhaps more importantly, *who we must become*.[7] And this brings us back to the truth of truths: you and I cannot enjoy the powers of God in our midst unless our lives are centered in the Son of God. We do not receive spiritual power from the universe; we receive it from the Christ.

It is the Christ-centered man or woman who enjoys the fruits of Christ's atoning work. It is the person who has obtained and retained a remission of sins—through the blood of Jesus shed in Gethsemane and on Golgotha—who is a fit vessel of the Lord's goodness and grace. While worthy and capable men and women are always active and involved in *the Church,* they are, more particularly, enjoying the sweet fruits of *the gospel* of Jesus Christ; it is the gospel that is the power of God unto salvation (Romans 1:16). And we prepare ourselves and our families and societies for the Second Coming most effectively when the image of Christ is in our countenances (Alma 5:14) and the testimony of Jesus is upon our lips.

The early Latter-day Saints, who were so often victims of the brutality of vicious men, were told: "Wherefore, be subject to the powers that be, until he reigns whose right it is to reign, and subdues all enemies under his feet" (D&C 58:22). We say again, Jesus Christ is coming to earth once again, not this time as the meek and lowly lamb but instead as the King of kings and Lord of lords. He is coming to reward those who have chosen him as Lord and Savior and to lay waste a world that has for far too long harbored the unclean and the ungodly. He is coming to bring in a day of righteousness, when the earth shall finally rest (Moses 7:48, 61). He is coming to earth again, this time to "restore again the kingdom to Israel" (Acts 1:6), to reconcile Judah with Ephraim, and to gather his sheep into one fold from all corners of the globe.

It is unlikely that you and I will live as mortals to see that day of glory and terror, that moment of rejoicing and remorse, but we have been charged to *live today* as if he were coming tomorrow—to live in readiness. Truly, the only answer to the world's ills is to have the gospel of Jesus Christ infused into the lives of all of us, and the only power by which we may be taught and baptized and sanctified is the power of the priesthood of God.

I yearn for that great day of deliverance. I long for the time when misery and pain and distress of soul will be no more, when happiness and joy are the order of the day. John the Revelator wrote: "He which testifieth these things saith, Surely I come quickly. Amen. Even so, *come, Lord Jesus.* The grace of our Lord Jesus Christ be with you all" (Revelation 22:20–21; emphasis added).

May God enable us, through his redeeming and purifying grace, to do our part to prepare the world for the glorious second advent of his Son, our Lord and King and Savior, Jesus Christ.

NOTES

PREFACE

1. "Master, the Tempest Is Raging," *Hymns*, no. 105.

CHAPTER 1: WHILE IT IS CALLED TODAY

1. "Jesus, Once of Humble Birth," *Hymns*, no. 196.
2. Smith, *Doctrines of Salvation*, 3:1.

CHAPTER 2: "UPON MY HOUSE SHALL IT BEGIN"

1. Packer, "The Mantle Is Far, Far Greater Than the Intellect," in *Let Not Your Heart Be Troubled*, 109–10.

CHAPTER 3: THE LOVE OF MEN WAXES COLD

1. Holland, *Christ and the New Covenant*, 336.
2. McKay, *Gospel Ideals*, 390.

CHAPTER 4: FALSE CHRISTS

1. This expression was used by President Joseph F. Smith to describe one of the categories of persons who have been deceived and misled (*Gospel Doctrine*, 373).
2. McConkie, *Millennial Messiah*, 48.

CHAPTER 5: THE PRECEPTS OF MEN

1. *Teachings of the Prophet Joseph Smith*, 205; see also Smith, *History of the Church* 4:573. This passage is from an article by the Prophet Joseph Smith entitled "Try the Spirits," *Times and Seasons* 3 (Apr. 1, 1842): 743–48.
2. Smith, *History of the Church*, 1:338.

3. *Teachings of the Prophet Joseph Smith*, 111; Smith, *History of the Church*, 2:477.

4. *Teachings of the Prophet Joseph Smith*, 256; Smith, *History of the Church*, 5:135.

5. McConkie, *Doctrines of the Restoration*, 67; emphasis added.

6. *Teachings of the Prophet Joseph Smith*, 203, 208–9; Smith, *History of the Church*, 4:572, 576.

7. *Teachings of the Prophet Joseph Smith*, 156–57; Smith, *History of the Church*, 3:385.

8. McConkie, *Millennial Messiah*, 70.

CHAPTER 6: "GO YE OUT FROM BABYLON"

1. Holland, "Sanctify Yourselves," *Ensign*, Nov. 2000, 39.

2. Andersen, "It's True, Isn't It? Then What Else Matters?" *Ensign*, May 2007, 74.

3. Webster, *American Dictionary of the English Language*, s.v. "Holy."

4. See Bork, *Slouching towards Gomorrah*.

5. Elder Dallin H. Oaks distinguished between what he called "intermediate judgments," which we must make every day, and "final judgments," which we have neither the data nor the insight to make (*With Full Purpose of Heart*, 191–195).

6. Packer, "These Things I Know," *Ensign*, May 2013, 8.

7. Smith, *Sharing the Gospel with Others*, 42–43.

CHAPTER 7: OUR LAMPS FILLED WITH OIL

1. Bednar, "Converted unto the Lord," *Ensign*, Nov. 2012, 109.

2. See *Lectures on Faith*, 38, 67–68.

3. Grant, *Journal of Discourses*, 4:18; emphasis added.

CHAPTER 8: TREASURING UP THE WORD

1. Smith, *History of the Church*, 4:540.

2. *Teachings of the Prophet Joseph Smith*, 296; Smith, *History of the Church*, 5:362.

3. Scott, "The Power of Scripture," *Ensign*, Nov. 2011, 6.

CHAPTER 9: STANDING IN HOLY PLACES

1. *Cowley and Whitney on Doctrine*, 287.

2. This truth is taught beautifully by C. S. Lewis in *Miracles*, 161–63.

3. Rasmussen, *Lord's Question*, 4; emphasis added.

4. Oaks, "The Challenge to Become," *Ensign*, Nov. 2000, 32–34.

5. Lee, Conference Report, April 1943, 129; emphasis added.

6. Rasmussen, *Lord's Question*, 7.

CHAPTER 10: LOOKING FORTH FOR THE GREAT DAY

1. McConkie, *Doctrinal New Testament Commentary*, 1:674–77; emphasis added.

2. Covey, *How to Succeed with People*, 93.

3. See McConkie, *Millennial Messiah*, 26–27, 405.

CHAPTER 12: CONFIDENT WHEN HE COMES

1. *Lectures on Faith*, 38.

2. McKay, *Gospel Ideals*, 390; emphasis added.

3. In Madsen, "Power from Abrahamic Tests," 49; emphasis added.

4. Holland, *Trusting Jesus*, 170–72.

CHAPTER 13: THE GOSPEL PREACHED IN ALL THE WORLD

1. McConkie, "The Coming Tests and Trials and Glory," *Ensign*, May 1980, 72.

2. See Packer, "The Bishop and His Counselors," *Ensign*, May 1999, 63.

3. McConkie, *Millennial Messiah*, 21–22.

4. *Teachings of the Prophet Joseph Smith*, 113; Smith, *History of the Church*, 2:478.

CHAPTER 14: "ISRAEL SHALL BE SAVED"

1. [Ballard], *Melvin J. Ballard*, 218–19.

2. McConkie, Conference Report, Mexico and Central America Area Conference, Aug. 1972, 43, 45.

3. Lee, "Strengthen the Stakes of Zion," *Ensign*, July 1973, 4–5.

4. See Packer, "To Be Learned Is Good If . . . ," *Ensign*, Nov. 1992, 71.

5. Holland, *For Times of Trouble*, DVD, which contains questions to Elder Holland and answers by him.

6. See Lee, "Be Loyal to the Royal within You," 100.

CHAPTER 15: WARS AND RUMORS OF WARS

1. McKay, Conference Report, April 1942, 70–73; emphasis in original.

2. Lee, *Ye Are the Light of the World*, 350–51; emphasis added.

CHAPTER 16: THE FALL OF BABYLON

1. Roberts, Conference Report, April 1906, 15.

2. Hunter, "Jesus, the Very Thought of Thee," *Ensign*, May 1993, 64–65; emphasis added.

3. See Smith, *Sharing the Gospel with Others*, 42–43.

CHAPTER 17: "MY PEOPLE WILL I PRESERVE"

1. *Teachings of the Prophet Joseph Smith*, 160, 161; Smith, *History of the Church*, 3:390, 91.
2. *Teachings of the Prophet Joseph Smith*, 162–63; Smith, *History of the Church*, 4:11.
3. McConkie, "Stand Independent above All Other Creatures," *Ensign*, May 1979, 93.

CHAPTER 18: THE NEW JERUSALEM

1. *Teachings of the Prophet Joseph Smith*, 183; Smith, *History of the Church*, 4:272.
2. First Presidency [Gordon B. Hinckley, Thomas S. Monson, James E. Faust], "The Family: A Proclamation to the World," *Ensign*, Nov. 2010, 129.
3. *Teachings of the Prophet Joseph Smith*, 160; Smith, *History of the Church*, 3:390.
4. McConkie, *Millennial Messiah*, 301–302; emphasis added.
5. See Benson, "Flooding the Earth with the Book of Mormon," *Ensign*, Nov. 1988, 4–6.
6. *Teachings of the Prophet Joseph Smith*, 84; Smith, *History of the Church*, 2:260; emphasis added.

CHAPTER 19: KNOWING THE SIGNS OF THE TIMES

1. Lee, "Admonitions for the Priesthood of God," *Ensign*, Jan. 1973, 106.
2. McConkie, *Millennial Messiah*, 251.
3. Ballard, "When Shall These Things Be?" 186; emphasis added.
4. Romney, "A Glorious Promise," *Ensign*, Jan. 1981, 2; emphasis added.
5. Holland, "My Words . . . Never Cease," *Ensign*, May 2008, 93.
6. See Smith, *Gospel Doctrine*, 116–17, 122.
7. Oaks, "Preparation for the Second Coming," *Ensign*, May 2004, 8–9.

CHAPTER 20: MEN AND WOMEN OF DESTINY

1. Oaks, "Preparation for the Second Coming," *Ensign*, May 2004, 9.
2. Monson, "To the Rescue," *Ensign*, May 2001, 48.
3. See Lee, "Stand Ye in Holy Places," *Ensign*, July 1973, 123.
4. *Teachings of the Prophet Joseph Smith*, 191; Smith, *History of the Church*, 4:425.
5. See *Discourses of Wilford Woodruff*, 5.
6. McKay, Conference Report, Oct. 1956, 91.
7. See Oaks, "The Challenge to Become," *Ensign*, Nov. 2000, 32–34.

GLOSSARY

Adam. Adam is the father of the human family, the first mortal on earth, and the one designated in scripture as the Ancient of Days (Daniel 7:22; D&C 27:11). He was Michael, the prince or archangel, in our first estate. He will preside at the council of Adam-ondi-Ahman. Under the direction of Jesus Christ, Adam will announce the resurrection and direct it (D&C 29:26).

Adam-ondi-Ahman. The site of one of the Savior's preliminary appearances prior to his coming in glory, Adam-ondi-Ahman will be the place where all those who have held the keys of the priesthood in the various dispensations will give an accounting to Adam (D&C 116:1). As the head of the human family, Adam will then account to Jesus Christ, whose right it will be to reign as King of kings and Lord of lords (Revelation 17:14; 19:16; D&C 58:22).

Antichrist. An antichrist is one who denies, defies, strives to oppose, and fights against the Lord Jesus Christ and his plan of redemption. This may be a person, an organization, or a false point of view.

Apocalypse. The word *apocalypse* means "uncovering, unveiling, revealing." Some characteristics of apocalyptic writing include symbolic numbers; strange creatures; astral phenomena, or signs in the heavens; cosmic dualism (day and night, black and white, good and evil, God and Satan); an overriding message to hold on. Satan may seem to be in charge for the time being, but the day is not far distant when the God of heaven will bring an end to evil and initiate an era of righteousness. While apocalyptic writings and themes are found in various books of scripture (Ezekiel, Daniel, Matthew 24, Mark 13, 1 Nephi 13–14), the Apocalypse, or the Revelation, of John the Beloved is the most comprehensive example of this prophetic genre.

Armageddon. Although the word *Armageddon* refers specifically to the hills of Megiddo and a battle in Israel that will take place just before our Lord's coming in glory, the name Armageddon is also used for the battle that will in fact be worldwide warfare (Revelation 16:14–16). On one side will be the forces of Satan, or the great and abominable church (2 Nephi 6:12; D&C 29:21) or mother of harlots (Revelation 13:34), and on the other side, the forces of righteousness, or the covenant people of the Lord (Acts 3:25; 1 Nephi 14:14) or the Church of the Lamb of God (1 Nephi 14:10, 12, 14).

Babylon. Ancient Babylon was a powerful nation that was a formidable, almost perennial, foe to the children of Israel. Over time, the word Babylon came to refer to evil influences and diabolical forces arrayed against the people of God (1 Peter 5:13; Revelation 14:8; 17:5; 18:2; D&C 1:16; 35:11; 64:24; 86:3; 133:5, 7, 14).

Bridegroom. In metaphoric terms, Jesus Christ is the Bridegroom (D&C 65:3) and the people of his Church are the bride (D&C 109:73–74). Just as in ancient times a bridegroom would journey with the wedding party to the home of his intended bride to convey her to the wedding, even so will the Lord Jesus Christ return to earth, with hosts of the righteous dead, to receive his Church and kingdom on earth. The wedding feast is a reunion between the people of the covenant and the Mediator of that covenant (Matthew 22:1–14; Luke 14:7–24).

Celestial kingdom. The celestial kingdom is the highest heaven, the noblest and grandest attainment hereafter to which the children of God can aspire. It will be composed of those who have the testimony of Jesus and have received the covenant gospel; have entered into the Lord's Church and kingdom by subscribing to the first principles and ordinances of the gospel; have sought to keep the commandments of God; have overcome the world through their faith in Jesus Christ; have been sealed by the Holy Spirit of Promise; have been received into the Church of the Firstborn; have become kings and queens, priests and priestesses unto God; and who have become gods, even the sons and daughters of God (D&C 76:51–58). In addition, it will be inhabited by those who did not have the opportunity to receive the fulness of the gospel in this life, who would have received it if they had had that opportunity, including children who died before the age of accountability (D&C 137:7–10). This earth, in its sanctified and glorified state, will become the celestial kingdom (D&C 88:15–20; 130:9).

Church of the Firstborn. The Church of the Firstborn is made up of those who qualify for eternal life. Whereas baptism is the means by which individuals are born again and received into the family of the Lord Jesus Christ, temple sealing and subsequent faithfulness to temple covenants is the means by which members of the Church become the sons and daughters of God the Father. They thereby become joint heirs or coinheritors with Christ to all the Father has (D&C 76:54–59, 71, 94–95). They qualify to inherit with Christ, who is the natural firstborn, as though they themselves were the firstborn (D&C 93:21–22).

Dispensation of the fulness of times. A dispensation is a period of time during which the fulness of the gospel, including the holy priesthood and knowledge of God's plan of salvation, are revealed and conferred through prophets to the children of the Father. We live now in the dispensation of the fulness of times, which is the last or final dispensation during the period of the earth's temporal continuance (D&C 27:13; 110:16). There will never again be a complete apostasy of the Lord's Church. This final dispensation is, as it were, the grand ocean of truth and power into which all the streams and rivers of past dispensations flow (D&C 121:26–32).

Elias. As described in latter-day revelation, Elias signifies a messenger or a forerunner, one who goes before and prepares the way. Just as John the Baptist prepared the way for the mortal Messiah and was thus an Elias in the meridian dispensation, even so Joseph Smith has prepared the way for the Savior's second coming and is an Elias in this final dispensation. Similarly, Elias can signify multiple messengers or angels. Moroni, for example, was the fulfillment of the prophecy of John concerning another angel flying through the midst of heaven having the everlasting gospel (Revelation 14:6–7); so also were John the Baptist, Peter, James, John, Moses, Elijah, Michael, Raphael, and hosts of heavenly ministrants (D&C 27:6–13; 128:21).

End of the earth. The end of the earth (D&C 38:5; 43:31; 88:101; Joseph Smith–Matthew 1:55) comes at the end of the thousand years we know as the Millennium. It is then that this planet will be celestialized.

End of the world. The end of the world is the destruction of the wicked (Matthew 24:3*b*; Joseph Smith–Matthew 1:4, 31), the end of worldliness that will happen at the time of the Savior's coming in glory, when he cleanses the earth by fire (2 Nephi 30:10; Jacob 6:3).

Endure to the end. To endure to the end is to keep our covenants until we have finished our work here on the earth—until we die. It is to leave this earth temple worthy and active and faithful in the Church. Those who endure to the end will receive eternal life, or salvation (1 Nephi 13:37; 22:31; 2 Nephi 31:15; 3 Nephi 27:6; D&C 6:13; 14:7; 50:5; 18:22; 101:35; see also *Salvation* in this glossary).

Eternal life. Eternal life is God's life, salvation in the highest degree of the celestial kingdom, a life reserved for those who receive the fulness of the power and glory of the Father (see also *Salvation* in this glossary).

Eternal lives. To have eternal lives is to have eternal life and to qualify for that life hereafter in which the family unit continues everlastingly. It is "to know the only wise and true God, and Jesus Christ, whom he hath sent" (D&C 132:24; compare John 17:3; see also D&C 132:22, 25, 30).

Eternal progression. The plan by which individuals grow and develop from the time they were spirits until they are glorified in the resurrection is often referred to as eternal progression. It is a system of faith that enables the children of God to gradually acquire the fruit of the Spirit (Galatians 5:22–25); to gain the mind of Christ (1 Corinthians 2:16); to come to embody and reflect charity, or the pure love of Christ (Moroni 7:47); and to see God as he is, for they will have become like him (1 John 3:1–3).

Exaltation. To receive exaltation is to qualify for life with God and with our family everlastingly. Salvation is a personal attainment; exaltation is a family affair (D&C 132:19–20; Benson, *Ensign,* Apr. 1993, 6).

False Christs. Other than those few deluded individuals who suppose they are Jesus or have some unnatural messiah complex, false Christs are false systems of salvation, false teachings or practices or lifestyles that lead one away from "peace in this world, and eternal life in the world to come" (D&C 59:23).

False prophets. False prophets are purveyors of false information, blind guides (Matthew 23:16), or those who teach the unwary to accept the precepts of men.

Fire and brimstone. Joseph Smith taught that "the torment of disappointment in the mind of man"—the realization of what we could have done and who we could have become and yet did not—"is as exquisite as a lake burning with fire and brimstone" (*Joseph Smith* [manual], 224; *Teachings of the Prophet Joseph Smith*, 357).

Gathering of Israel. Individuals are gathered when they accept the true Messiah, his gospel, his Church, and his doctrine and congregate with the faithful. One of the signs of the times is that the children of Israel will begin to be gathered into the Church and kingdom of God in greater and greater numbers as the time is accelerated preparatory to the ushering in of the Millennium (1 Nephi 15:13–16; 2 Nephi 6:8–11; 9:1–2; 10:3–7). The gathering is accomplished through missionary work, as "one of a city, and two of a family" (Jeremiah 3:14) are taught the principles of the restored gospel and receive baptism and confirmation and the blessings of the temple at the hands of authorized administrators. People participate in the final phase of the gathering as they receive the covenants and ordinances of the temple (*Joseph Smith* [manual], 416–17; *Teachings of the Prophet Joseph Smith*, 307–8; *History of the Church*, 5:423)

Gentile. In one sense, a person is a Gentile who is not a descendant of Abraham or one of the twelve sons of Jacob. In a broader, scriptural sense, a Gentile is someone from "the nations," meaning a nation or country outside the Holy Land (Jeremiah 16:19a; Matthew 12:21b; 1 Nephi 22:6–11; 2 Nephi 30:3–4). In that sense, most Latter-day Saints are Israelite by covenant but Gentile by culture or nation (1 Nephi 22:7–8; D&C 109:60).

Gentiles, times of the. Jesus taught that the first shall be last and the last shall be first (Matthew 19:30; 20:16; 1 Nephi 13:42; Jacob 5:63). This teaching has to do with the order in which the gospel is presented to the children of men. In the meridian of time, the gospel went first to the Jews and then to the Gentiles (Matthew 10:5–6; 15:24). In our day the gospel was restored through a great Gentile nation (1 Nephi 22:7–8) and will eventually go to all the children of Israel. The times of the Gentiles is that day when the gospel of Jesus Christ comes first to and through those denominated as Gentiles, meaning cultural Gentiles. The fulness of the times of the Gentiles is that time when the Gentiles will have rejected and sinned against the fulness of the gospel and thus disqualified themselves from its benefits and blessings. The gospel will then, for example, be taken from the Gentiles and given to the Jews (3 Nephi 16:10–11; D&C 45:24–25).

Godhood. One of the grand and transcendent purposes of the gospel of Jesus Christ is to sanctify and transform the children of God, to prepare them not only to dwell with God hereafter but also to be like him. To be like God is to be Christlike, to embody the fruit of the Spirit (Galatians 5:19–25), and to live and interact as did our Master, the prototype of all saved beings, when he dwelt on earth. To attain godhood is to become perfect (whole, complete, mature; Matthew 5:48b) in and through Christ (Moroni 10:32); to become a joint heir with Christ (Romans 8:14–18; D&C 76:68); to be a partaker of the divine nature (2 Peter 1:2–4); and to become, by spiritual regeneration, the sons or daughters of God. These are they who are gods (D&C 76:58).

Gog and Magog, battle of. The final great battle between the forces of evil and the forces of good, between Satan and God, between Lucifer and Michael, is called the battle of Gog and Magog. It takes place at the end of the Millennium (*Teachings of the Prophet Joseph Smith*, 280; *History of the Church*, 5:298). After this war of words and immense struggle of ideas, after Satan is dismissed and banished from earth forevermore (Revelation 20:7–10), the earth will be sanctified and become the celestial kingdom.

Great and abominable church. The great and abominable church (1 Nephi 13:5), the church of the devil, the whore of all the earth (1 Nephi 14:10), or the mother of harlots (1 Nephi 13:34) is that organization of evil, that consortium of corruption, that fights against Zion, denies and defies the work of the Lord and the Lord himself (2 Nephi 10:16). It is any organization—social, economic, political, fraternal, philosophical, or religious—that secretly or openly opposes righteousness in the earth and the establishment of the kingdom of God. Eventually those persons and organizations who make up the church of the devil will turn upon themselves, and Babylon will fall (Revelation 18; 1 Nephi 22:13–14, 22–23).

Heaven. The traditional Christian world holds that there are only two possible states or conditions that a person will enjoy when he or she leaves this life: heaven or hell. But Jesus explained that "in my Father's house are many mansions" (John 14:2). The apostle Paul taught that there are different types of bodies in the resurrection, dependent upon what level of righteousness a person chose in mortality to pursue (JST 1 Corinthians 15:40–42). The Prophet Joseph Smith learned by vision (D&C 76) that there are more heavens than one hereafter—celestial, terrestrial, and telestial. With the exception of those who defect to perdition, God will save all of his children in a kingdom of glory (D&C 76:31–39).

Hell. At the moment individuals breathe their last, they enter the postmortal spirit world. There each experiences a partial judgment and takes up residence either in paradise (the righteous), or in what the scriptures call hell or outer darkness (the wicked), or in what is sometimes called spirit prison, the abode of those who have yet to learn the gospel (1 Peter 3:18–20; 2 Nephi 9:10–12; Alma 40:11–14). At the time of the second, or last, resurrection (the resurrection of telestial persons and sons of perdition), the spirit world is emptied (2 Nephi 9:12), and all are resurrected (Alma 11:41). Except for the sons of perdition, who inherit an eternal outer darkness (D&C 76:33, 37–38), hell will be no more.

Holy Spirit of Promise. The Holy Spirit of Promise is the Holy Ghost, the Holy Spirit promised to the Saints. This third member of the Godhead is a comforter, a teacher, a testifier, a sanctifier, and a sealer. Because he knows all things (D&C 42:17; Moses 6:61), the Comforter is able to search the minds and hearts of all people and determine those who have obeyed the truth and sought after goodness and righteousness. The Spirit certifies that such a person is a just man or woman and worthy of eternal life. He ratifies, or approves, all covenants and ordinances a person has received (baptism, confirmation, ordination for men, endowment, and sealing) and places an eternal stamp upon that life.

Immortality. To receive immortality is to live in a resurrected condition forever. What the Savior makes available to us is resurrected, glorified immortality in the presence of God and the Lamb (2 Nephi 9:13–14, 18).

Joint heirs with Christ. Those who receive the gospel covenant with its attendant ordinances become the sons and daughters of the

Lord Jesus Christ by adoption (Mosiah 5:7; Ether 3:14). Those who thereafter receive the ordinances of the temple and keep their covenants become the sons and daughters of God, meaning the Father (Mosiah 27:25; D&C 11:30; 76:58; Moses 7:1). They become joint heirs, or coinheritors, with Christ of all the Father has (Romans 8:17; D&C 76:55).

Judgment Day. The children of God pass through a series of judgments throughout their lives. At the time of death, individuals undergo a partial judgment (Alma 40:11–13). When individuals are resurrected, they experience a kind of judgment in being raised with a body adapted to the kingdom of glory each will inherit—celestial, terrestrial, or telestial (D&C 76:28–31). The Final Judgment, which Christians refer to as Judgment Day, comes after the second, or last, resurrection.

Lost tribes of Israel. The ten northern tribes of Israel were scattered throughout the nations after the Assyrian conquest in 721 B.C., and became known as the lost tribes of Israel (1 Nephi 22:3–4). Through the generations that followed, persons and groups who chose to follow Jehovah and associate with the people of the covenant were gathered, first spiritually (to the Lord and his gospel) and then temporally (to the lands of their inheritance). As time moves on toward the day when Jesus Christ will return in glory, the missionary efforts of The Church of Jesus Christ of Latter-day Saints will intensify, and members of the house of Israel whose lineal descent is from those tribes who were once a part of the northern tribes will come into the Church through baptism, gather with the Saints in the congregations where they reside, receive the ordinances of the temple, endure faithfully to the end of their lives, and thereby qualify for eternal life. The gathering of the ten tribes—the keys of which are held by the president of the Church (D&C 110:11)—is largely a millennial endeavor (2 Nephi 30:7–15; 3 Nephi 21:25–26).

Millennium. When Jesus Christ returns in power and glory, the Millennium begins (D&C 29:11). It will be a thousand years of peace and rest, joy and happiness, freedom from the woes and waywardness of our present telestial world. The earth and the mortals who inhabit it will be raised to a terrestrial level of glory. The Millennium will be brought in by the cleansing and renovating power of the Savior, and it will be maintained by the righteousness of the people (1 Nephi 22:15, 26).

Mountain of the Lord's house. A scriptural phrase that refers to the connecting links between God and man, the mountain of the Lord's house represents the high and holy places we know as temples, or houses, of the Lord (Isaiah 2:2–3; compare D&C 84:2– 4). Temples link time and eternity, past, present, and future, the living and the dead, husbands and wives, parents and children, and each individual to Christ.

A new heaven and a new earth. When Jesus returns in glory, the earth, together with its heavenly surroundings, will be "renewed and receive its paradisiacal glory" (Articles of Faith 1:10). That is, it will be raised to a terrestrial glory. At the end of the Millennium, the earth will be raised to a celestial glory and thereby prepared for those will receive eternal life and exaltation to inhabit it (D&C 56:18–20). And so, once again, there will be a new heaven and a new earth (Isaiah 65:17; Revelation 21:1; D&C 29:23).

Olivet prophecy. During the last week of his mortal life, the Savior took his apostles to the Mount of Olives and there set forth many of the signs of the times—the events leading up to his coming in glory (false Christs, false prophets, wars and rumors of wars, men's hearts failing them, gospel preached to all the world, and so forth). Both Matthew 24 and Mark 13 present these signs in an orderly fashion. Joseph Smith's translation of Matthew 24 (which is reflected in JST Mark 13) is more comprehensive, more systematic, and far more insightful than those in other versions of the Bible, even the King James. Joseph Smith's translation of these chapters may well be our most complete prophetic expression of what lies ahead.

One hundred forty-four thousand. Modern revelation provides insight into the rather enigmatic group referred to in chapters 7 and 14 of John's Revelation. These one hundred forty-four thousand persons are high priests after the holy order of God, men who have the assignment to "bring as many as will come to the church of the Firstborn" (D&C 77:11). Their role is to make available to individuals throughout the earth the fulness of the blessings of the priesthood, thereby sealing up unto eternal life the Saints of the Most High. More than anything else, this number is a prophetic statement that temples will dot the earth, that all the blessings of those temples will be available to an ever-expanding number of God's children.

Outer darkness. See *Hell* in this glossary.

Paradise. See *Hell* in this glossary.

Paradisiacal glory. See *A new heaven and a new earth* in this glossary.

Perdition, son of. Joseph Smith explained that in order for a person to commit the unpardonable sin and thereby become a son of perdition, that person must "receive the Holy Ghost, have the heavens opened . . . , and know God, and then sin against Him" (*Teachings of the Prophet Joseph Smith*, 358; *History of the Church*, 6:314). Sons of perdition are persons who have enjoyed an unusual outpouring of spiritual light and understanding and then choose to deny the faith and fight the work of the Lord. They blaspheme against the Holy Ghost (Matthew 12:31–32) and shed anew the innocent blood of Christ (Hebrews 6:4–6; 10:26–29; D&C 76:28–35). Sons of perdition are the only ones who will be subject to the second, or final, spiritual death and inherit a kingdom of no glory (D&C 76:36–39; 132:27).

Priesthood, fulness of. The fulness of the blessings of the priesthood are to be had only through the covenants and ordinances of the temple (D&C 124:48). Those who receive the fulness of the priesthood are kings and queens, priests and priestesses unto God in the house of Israel (Revelation 1:6; D&C 76:56; *Joseph Smith* [manual], 109; *Teachings of the Prophet Joseph Smith*, 322; *History of the Church*, 5:555).

The rest of the Lord. The scriptures speak often of how the faithful may enter into the rest of the Lord, or God (Alma 12:34–37; 13:12). Entering into the rest of God takes place when a person is living the gospel and gains the peace associated with a settled conviction of the truth (Moroni 7:3); when a person dies firm in the faith, passes through the veil of death, and takes up residence in paradise (Alma 40:12); when a person enters the presence of the Lord (D&C 84:24; JST Exodus 34:2); or when a person is admitted into heaven (Moroni 7:3), what we know as the celestial kingdom.

Resurrection. Just as death is the separation of the spirit from the body, so resurrection is the reuniting of the spirit and body into an inseparable union (2 Nephi 9:13; Alma 11:43; 40:23). The embodied spirit constitutes the soul of man, and the resurrection is the redemption of that soul (D&C 88:15–16). A fulness of joy comes only through the resurrection (D&C 93:33). Jesus Christ broke the bands of death and was raised from the tomb into celestial, resurrected glory, and because he rose, we have the assurance that each and every mortal will thereby enjoy the immortality of the soul (1 Corinthians 15:21–22; Alma 11:40–42).

Resurrection, first. The first resurrection is the resurrection of those who inherit either celestial or terrestrial glory (Mosiah 15:21–22). The first resurrection, which was initiated in the meridian of time by Jesus Christ, will resume when the Savior returns in glory and will continue throughout the Millennium.

Resurrection, last (second). The second, or last, resurrection is the resurrection of those who inherit the telestial glory and those who inherit a kingdom of no glory, the sons of perdition (D&C 76:81–106; 88:32–35). The second resurrection takes place after the Millennium.

Salvation. To gain salvation, in the scriptural sense, is to gain eternal life (Alma 11:40–42; D&C 6:13; 14:7). To be saved is to be healed spiritually, to be delivered from death, hell, the devil, and endless torment (Mosiah 16:11). Joseph Smith taught that to be saved is to triumph over all our enemies and put them under our feet (*Joseph Smith* [manual], 212; *Teachings of the Prophet Joseph Smith*, 297; *History of the Church*, 5:387). "Salvation consists in the glory, authority, majesty, power and dominion which Jehovah possesses and in nothing else; and no being can possess it but himself or one like him" (*Lectures on Faith*, 76; see also *Exaltation* in this glossary).

Scattering of Israel. The people of Israel, as individuals or as a nation, are scattered when they reject the true Messiah, the gospel covenant, his doctrine, and his Church (2 Nephi 6:8–11; 10:3–7). Israel is scattered also when God chooses, in his eternal wisdom, to relocate a branch of Israel (such as the Lehite colony) so that the promises made to Abraham, Isaac, and Jacob that their posterity would be found throughout the earth and be a blessing to the world may be fulfilled (1 Nephi 17:36–38; 2 Nephi 1:5; 10:20–22).

Sea of glass. The sea of glass spoken of by John in Revelation 4:6 is "the earth, in its sanctified, immortal, and eternal state" (D&C 77:1). It is not that those who inherit the celestial kingdom will literally live on glass but rather that the earth will become like a great

Urim and Thummim (D&C 130:9). That is, those who inhabit the sanctified earth will be "full of the knowledge of the Lord, as the waters cover the sea" (Isaiah 11:9; Habakkuk 2:14).

Second Comforter. The First Comforter is the Holy Ghost, the third member of the Godhead, the One sent of the Father as a comforter, revelator, testator, sanctifier, and sealer (John 14:26; D&C 36:2; 42:17; 50:14). The Second Comforter is the second member of the Godhead, the Lord Jesus Christ himself (John 14:16; *Teachings of the Prophet Joseph Smith,* 149–50; *History of the Church,* 3:381). When a person receives the Second Comforter, he or she is brought into the presence of the Lord. We have been taught that such a transcendent privilege, though rare, is possible in this life (D&C 67:10–13; 76:114–118; 88:68; 93:1). Until that glorious day, we are instructed to "seek the face of the Lord always, that in patience ye may possess your souls, and ye shall have eternal life" (D&C 101:38). Inasmuch as the Savior will dwell with the people on earth during the thousand years of peace and joy (3 Nephi 20:22; 21:25), the Millennium is in very deed the day of the Second Comforter.

The Second Coming. Although the Lord Jesus Christ will come to earth to visit his people several times before the Millennium, we usually speak of the Second Coming as the occasion when he comes to all in glory, in might and majesty and power (Matthew 16:27). He will cleanse the earth of sin and inaugurate an era of peace and righteousness (2 Thessalonians 2:8).

Second comings. Three preliminary comings of the Savior to the earth are spoken of in scripture: his appearance at his temple in Independence, Missouri (Malachi 3:1; D&C 36:8; 42:35–36; 133:2); his appearance at the council of Adam-ondi-Ahman (D&C 116); and his appearance to the Jews on the Mount of Olives (Zechariah 12:10; 13:6; D&C 45:47–53). And surely there will be other visits, even many visits, to prepare the earth and the Saints of the Most High for their glorious transfiguration.

Spirit prison. See *Hell* in this glossary.

Telestial kingdom. The telestial kingdom is the lowest of the three degrees of glory. It will be made up of those who received neither the testimony of Jesus nor the gospel covenant (D&C 76:82, 101), persons who were disobedient, who were liars, adulterers, sorcerers, and murderers, and who defied the laws of morality and decency (D&C 76:103). Those who inherit the glory of the telestial kingdom will have spent the Millennium being cleansed of their sins and made ready for this lowest kingdom of glory, whose glory "surpasses all understanding" (D&C 76:89).

Terrestrial kingdom. The terrestrial kingdom is likened to the glory of the moon in contrast to the celestial kingdom, which is likened to the glory of the sun (D&C 76:78). Those who inherit the terrestrial kingdom are they "who received not the testimony of Jesus in the flesh, but afterwards [in the postmortal spirit world] received it"; because they are not then "valiant in the testimony of Jesus," they do not qualify for a celestial crown (D&C 76:74, 79). Inhabitants of the terrestrial kingdom will thus include the honorable men and women of the earth who lived the best lives they knew to live, but because they were not valiant in the testimony of Jesus, they do not qualify for the richer blessings associated with living the celestial law.

Transfiguration of the earth. When Christ returns in glory, the earth and all who abide his presence will be transfigured, raised to a higher spiritual plane for a season (D&C 63:20–21). More specifically, they are raised from a telestial state to a terrestrial glory (Articles of Faith 1:10).

Translated beings. The Prophet Joseph Smith taught that translated beings, such as Enoch, Moses, Elijah, John the Beloved, and the Three Nephites, have been raised to a terrestrial order (*Teachings of the Prophet Joseph Smith*, 170). As such, they are not subject to death, pain, or distress. Because they have not yet passed through death and the resurrection, they are still mortal, albeit in a glorified mortal condition (3 Nephi 28:37–40).

Zion. Zion is the highest order of priesthood society and the abode of the pure in heart (D&C 97:21), which is any place where the pure in heart dwell. Although the center stake of Zion, or the New Jerusalem, will be established in Independence, Jackson County, Missouri (D&C 57:3), Zion will be everywhere a stake is formed and operating. At the time of the Lord's coming in glory, the Zion from above (Enoch's Zion, as well as all other Zions that have been taken from the earth; Moses 7:31) will unite with Zion on earth in a grand and sacred reunion (D&C 84:100; Moses 7:62–65).

SOURCES

Andersen, Neil L. "It's True, Isn't It? Then What Else Matters?" *Ensign*, May 2007, 74–75.

[Ballard, Melvin R.] *Melvin J. Ballard—Crusader for Righteousness*. Salt Lake City: Bookcraft, 1966.

Ballard, M. Russell. "When Shall These Things Be?" *Brigham Young University 1995–96 Speeches*, 185–93. Provo, Utah: Brigham Young University, 1996.

Bednar, David A. "Converted unto the Lord." *Ensign*, Nov. 2012, 106–9.

Benson, Ezra Taft. "Flooding the Earth with the Book of Mormon." *Ensign*, Nov. 1988, 4–6.

———. "Because I Live, Ye Shall Live Also." *Ensign*, Apr. 1993, 2–6.

Bork, Robert H. *Slouching towards Gomorrah: Modern Liberalism and American Decline*. New York: Harper Perennial, 2003.

Covey, Stephen R. *How to Succeed with People*. Salt Lake City: Deseret Book, 1971.

Cowley, Matthias, and Orson F. Whitney. *Cowley and Whitney on Doctrine*. Compiled by Forace Green. Salt Lake City: Bookcraft, 1963.

First Presidency [Gordon B. Hinckley, Thomas S. Monson, James E. Faust]. "The Family: A Proclamation to the World." *Ensign*, Nov. 2010, 129.

Hinckley, Gordon B. *Teachings of Gordon B. Hinckley*. Salt Lake City: Deseret Book, 1997.

Holland, Jeffrey R. *Christ and the New Covenant: The Messianic Message of the Book of Mormon*. Salt Lake City: Deseret Book, 1997.

————. *For Times of Trouble: Spiritual Solace from the Psalms*. Salt Lake City: Deseret Book, 2012.

————. "My Words . . . Never Cease." *Ensign*, May 2008, 91–94.

————. "Sanctify Yourselves." *Ensign*, Nov. 2000, 38–40.

————. *Trusting Jesus*. Salt Lake City: Deseret Book, 2003.

Hunter, Howard W. "Jesus, the Very Thought of Thee." *Ensign*, May 1993, 63–65.

Hymns of The Church of Jesus Christ of Latter-day Saints. Salt Lake City: The Church of Jesus Christ of Latter-day Saints, 1985.

Journal of Discourses. 26 vols. Liverpool: F. D. Richards & Sons, 1854–86.

Lectures on Faith. Salt Lake City: Deseret Book, 1985.

Lee, Harold B. "Admonitions for the Priesthood of God." *Ensign*, Jan. 1973, 104–8.

————. "Be Loyal to the Royal within You." *1973 Brigham Young University Speeches of the Year*, 85–104. Provo: BYU Publications, 1974.

————. Conference Report, Apr. 1943, 124–30.

————. "Stand Ye in Holy Places." *Ensign*, July 1973, 121–24.

————. "Strengthen the Stakes of Zion." *Ensign*, July 1973, 2–6.

————. *Ye Are the Light of the World*. Salt Lake City: Deseret Book, 1974.

Lewis, C. S. *Miracles: A Preliminary Study*. New York: Touchstone, 1996.

Madsen, Truman G. "Power from Abrahamic Tests." In *The Highest in Us*, 49–58. Salt Lake City: Bookcraft, 1978.

McConkie, Bruce R. "The Coming Tests and Trials and Glory." *Ensign*, May 1980, 71–73.

————. Conference Report, Mexico and Central America Area Conference, Aug. 1972, 41–46.

————. *Doctrinal New Testament Commentary*. 3 vols. Salt Lake City: Bookcraft, 1965–73.

————. *Doctrines of the Restoration: Sermons and Writings of Bruce R. McConkie*. Edited by Mark L. McConkie. Salt Lake City: Bookcraft, 1989.

————. *The Millennial Messiah: The Second Coming of the Son of Man*. Salt Lake City: Deseret Book, 1982.

———. *The Mortal Messiah: From Bethlehem to Calvary*. 4 vols. Salt Lake City: Deseret Book, 1979–81.

———. "Stand Independent above All Other Creatures." *Ensign*, May 1979, 92–94.

McKay, David O. Conference Report, Apr. 1942, 70–74.

———. Conference Report, Oct. 1956, 88–91.

———. *Gospel Ideals*. Salt Lake City: Improvement Era, 1953.

Monson, Thomas S. *Teachings of Thomas S. Monson*. Compiled by Lynne F. Cannegieter. Salt Lake City: Deseret Book, 2011.

———. "To the Rescue." *Ensign*, May 2001, 48–50.

Oaks, Dallin H. "The Challenge to Become." *Ensign*, Nov. 2000, 32–34.

———. "Preparation for the Second Coming." *Ensign*, May 2004, 7–10.

———. *With Full Purpose of Heart*. Salt Lake City: Deseret Book, 2002.

Packer, Boyd K. "The Bishop and His Counselors." *Ensign*, May 1999, 57–58, 63.

———. *Let Not Your Heart Be Troubled*. Salt Lake City: Bookcraft, 1991.

———. "These Things I Know." *Ensign*, May 2013, 6–8.

———. *The Things of the Soul*. Salt Lake City: Bookcraft, 1996.

———. "To Be Learned Is Good If . . ." *Ensign*, Nov. 1992, 71–73.

Rasmussen, Dennis. *The Lord's Question: Thoughts on the Life of Response*. Provo: Keter Foundation, 1985.

Roberts, B. H. In Conference Report, Apr. 1906, 13–17.

Romney, Marion G. "A Glorious Promise." *Ensign*, Jan. 1981, 2–3.

Scott, Richard G. "The Power of Scripture." *Ensign*, Nov. 2011, 6–8.

Smith, George Albert. *Sharing the Gospel with Others*. Salt Lake City: Deseret Book, 1948.

Smith, Joseph. *History of The Church of Jesus Christ of Latter-day Saints*. Edited by B. H. Roberts. 2d ed. rev. 7 vols. Salt Lake City: Deseret Book, 1972.

———. *Joseph Smith* [manual]. Teachings of the Presidents of the Church series. Salt Lake City: The Church of Jesus Christ of Latter-day Saints, 2007.

———. *Teachings of the Prophet Joseph Smith*. Selected by Joseph Fielding Smith. Salt Lake City: Deseret Book, 1967.

Smith, Joseph F. *Gospel Doctrine*. Salt Lake City: Deseret Book, 1986.

Smith, Joseph Fielding. *Doctrines of Salvation*. 3 vols. Compiled by Bruce R. McConkie. Salt Lake City: Bookcraft, 1954–56.

———. *The Progress of Man*. Salt Lake City: Deseret Book, 1964.

———. *The Way to Perfection*. Salt Lake City: Deseret Book, 1970.

Webster, Noah. *An American Dictionary of the English Language*. 1828. Reprint, San Francisco: Foundation for American Christian Education, 1985.

Woodruff, Wilford. *Discourses of Wilford Woodruff*. Selected by G. Homer Durham. Salt Lake City: Bookcraft, 1946.

SCRIPTURE INDEX

SUBJECT INDEX

146 ~ SUBJECT INDEX

Repentance, 7, 48, 58
Rest of the Lord, 128
Restoration, 101, 106–7
Resurrection, 128–29
Revelation, 23–26, 107–8
Righteousness, 81–84, 86–89, 93–96.
  See also Good/Goodness
Roberts, B. H., 87
Romney, Marion G., 107
Russia, missionary work in, 69

Salvation, 73–79, 112–13, 122, 129
Scattering of Israel, 75, 129
Scott, Richard G., 44
Scriptures, 36–37, 42–44, 105–7
Sea of glass, 129–30
Second Comforter, 130
Second Coming: timing of, 2–3, 106;
  preparing for, 3–4, 52–53, 108–14;
  looking forward to, 51–55; fear of,
  62–63, 92–96; signs of, 72, 103–9;
  defined, 130. See also Preparing for
  Second Coming
Second comings, 130
Second resurrection, 129
Self-discovery class, 16–18
Selfishness, 80
Signs of Second Coming, 72, 103–9
Sin, 7–8, 48, 30–31
Smith, George Albert, 31
Smith, Joseph: on false spirits, 23; on
  revelation, 23, 25; on finding fault
  with Church, 25–26; memorizing
  words of, 43; on faith, 63–64; on
  stakes of Zion, 94; on preservation
  of Saints, 94–95; on temporal and
  spiritual blessings, 97; on Zion, 99,
  102; on torment of disappointment,
  123; on sons of perdition, 128; on
  salvation, 129

Smith, Joseph Fielding, 2–3
Sociality, 97–98
Spirit prison. See Hell
Spirituality, 33–35; David O. McKay
  on, 64
Spiritual power, 61
Suffering, as part of discipleship, 5

Telestial kingdom, 130–31
Television, profanity and nudity in, 11
Temple implements, 27–28
Temples, 127
Temptation, 31
Ten virgins, parable of, 35–36, 40
Terrestrial kingdom, 130–31
Testimony, bearing, 111–12
Times of the Gentiles, 123–24
Timing of Second Coming, 2–3, 106
Tolerance, 29–31
Top, Brent, 30
Transfiguration of the earth, 131
Translated beings, 83, 98–99, 131
Trials, as part of discipleship, 5
Truth, discernment of, 23–26

Vigilance, 57

War, 80–85, 88–89
Wayward children, 77–79, 111–12
Wheat and tares, parable of, 8–9
White clothing, 57–58, 60
Whitney, Orson F., 46
Whore of all the earth, 87–90, 124
Will of God, compliance with, 63–64
Word of God, treasuring up, 41–45
World, 14–15, 28–29, 49, 122. See also
  Earth
Worthiness, for revelation, 24

Zion, 76–77, 94–96, 98–102, 131.
  See also New Jerusalem